Songs to Fill the Air:
Tales of the Grateful Dead

Scott W. Allen

Cover Illustrator

Steve Johannsen

Editor

Erik Anderson

Interior Illustrator

Hannah Hopkins

Songs to Fill the Air:
Tales of the Grateful Dead
All Rights Reserved.
Copyright © 2018 Scott W. Allen
v3.0

The opinions expressed in this manuscript are solely the opinions of the author and do not represent the opinions or thoughts of the publisher. The author has represented and warranted full ownership and/or legal right to publish all the materials in this book.

This book may not be reproduced, transmitted, or stored in whole or in part by any means, including graphic, electronic, or mechanical without the express written consent of the publisher except in the case of brief quotations embodied in critical articles and reviews.

Outskirts Press, Inc.
http://www.outskirtspress.com

ISBN: 978-1-4787-9128-7

Library of Congress Control Number: 2017913916

Cover Illustration © 2018 Steve Johannsen. All rights reserved - used with permission. Inquiries welcome:
JohannsenStudio@gmail.com

Interior Illustrations © 2018 Hannah Hopkins. All rights reserved - used with permission.
Inquiries welcome:
RockMySoulArt@gmail.com
GiveAPaintBrush@gmail.com

Outskirts Press and the "OP" logo are trademarks belonging to Outskirts Press, Inc.

PRINTED IN THE UNITED STATES OF AMERICA

"Without love in the dream it will never come true."

— Robert Hunter

table of contents

set one 1

set two 95

encores 139

set one

January 8, 1979

Before my younger brother Chris and I had ever laid eyes and ears on the Grateful Dead, we had seen well over 100 concerts — including the likes of the Rolling Stones, Jethro Tull, Pink Floyd, the Allmans, Paul McCartney, Boston, Aerosmith opening for Sabbath, Yes, Led Zeppelin and the Who, to name a few — dating to 1973, mostly in Manhattan, and nearly all at Madison Square Garden or the Palladium (the old Academy of Music) on E. 14th Street.

We were city kids, Bronx-born and raised. I was all of 19 and Chris was just 17 when we decided to catch our first Dead show — at the Garden on December 1, 1978. We'd been smoking pot for more than three years while also dabbling with psychoactives such as mescaline and MDMA. Tickets were $11 apiece, or less than what one currently pays in service charges for a single ticket.

While in high school, I was lucky enough to have the dream job of working at a record store — The Music Scene in White Plains. What a great way to meet girls when you're 17 ! The manager, an affable long-haired hippie-type named Hank, would make me go through the racks each day to learn every band's catalog. It was a task I loved, and I would gleefully, and methodically, spend hours familiarizing myself with the works of Be Bop Deluxe, Gentle Giant and some new cat named Prince.

I recall the day I came to the Grateful Dead's beefy section and, as I thumbed through their albums, telling myself, "This is one band I will *never* be into."

College was the gamechanger for me. I had attended a private high school run like a boot camp and by the start of my sophomore year in the fall of 1978 at Fordham University in the Bronx, New York, I realized I needed to let loose and find some new friends who loved music as much as I did, could party a bit, and hung out with pretty ladies. I ended up catching on with a crew who were wild about partying and dancing. Inevitably, at the end of each drunken night, we'd end up in someone's dorm suite, drinking beer and dancing as we beat on pots and pans to the tune of a music that was unfamiliar to my ears. Late one evening, I asked my friend TJ Healey the name of the band we were listening to. He replied, "The Grateful Dead and they're coming to the Garden in December."

The Garden wasn't like a second home to Chris and I. It was our second home.

Out front on Seventh Avenue, there was always a lively street scene — colorful scalpers (who weren't quite as scummy back then) with names like Slick Rick, Little Lenny, Ralphie Rip-Off and Carmine from the Bronx. There were also street dealers who had both real and bogus weed, hash and MDMA. Adding to the soft parade: the Button Man, an Asian with long black hair who sold buttons with color images of rock stars on them for $5 each. Interns from then-rock radio station WPLJ-FM — 95.5 — were always on Seventh Avenue handing out commemorative buttons featuring that night's headliners.

Today, those WPLJ buttons are worth a pretty penny on eBay.

The concert on December 1 had to be rescheduled to January 8, 1979 after Jerry came down with bronchitis and pneumonia. Chris and I had decided January 8 would not only be our first Dead show but also our first venture on acid. I'm not sure if we were more excited to see the band or trip. We were young and curious and, without second thought, dismissed the advice of the young Carlos Santana lookalike acid dealer under the Garden marquee who told us, "These are Full Moons, 200 mics each. You only need a half each, especially if it's your first time."

Let it not be said we weren't warned.

Nonchalantly, we each washed down a Full Moon with a swig of Tango, which tasted like the breakfast drink Tang mixed with backwoods gut rot, brashly asking one another with a guffaw: *What power could such a tiny piece of paper possibly possess ?*

We walked in just as the Dead broke into their opening song, "Mississippi Half-Step Uptown Toodeloo." I was immediately struck by the sense of motion permeating both the crowd and the music, each seemingly surfing a never-cresting wave that, from time-to-time, would peak in a shared band-audience orgasm — from the first song to the last ! Also remarkable to me: the fans stood all night and only sat down to meet or talk with other fans, roll a joint, or take a swig from a wine sack, which was then passed among people who didn't seem to know each other. There was a social element to the audience that I had never experienced at a concert before; at times, to "the Deadheads," conversation and socializing seemed more important than the music.

Chris and I were used to seeing Deadheads — easily identifiable by their long hair, tie dyes and clouds of pot smoke — at the Garden for shows by the likes of Neil Young and Crazy Horse, the Who and Zeppelin. They would discreetly sit in the back rows of the back sections of the Garden, where they would dance their dance. I admired their "could-care-less" attitude: They unabashedly danced, drank beer, lit up joints and had a grand ol' time.

I also respected their "tribalness," but remember thinking I could never see myself as one. I was into David Bowie, the Who, the Stones, T. Rex, Mott the Hoople and some of the new kids on the block: the Talking Heads, Elvis Costello, Television ...

To my surprise, the Garden ushers had already given up the fight to get the crowd to extinguish their joints and cigarettes. At a recent Cat Stevens concert, I had seen a kid have his ticket torn up by an usher and get hauled out by the scruff of his neck for sneaking a quick hit on a joint.

That was not going to happen tonight.

SET ONE

I was tripping good. Really good. The Garden walls were undulating, like taffy being churned in a stainless-steel vat, dripping with sweat generated by the white light /white heat coming from the stage. We met up with a handful of my college friends, who weren't tripping but were knocking down beer as if it were legal to do so at age 18 (which, in 1979, it was, thankfully).

The music was alive, a life force coursing with energy being created by a symbiotic relationship between the band and audience. It was unlike anything I had experienced before in a live music setting.

At halftime, Chris and I were tripping so hard that we remained glued to our seats, seatbelts tightly fastened, permanent grins etched on our faces, neither able to talk, let alone risk a trip to the bathroom or a concession stand.

All we really wanted was for the music to start again.

Finally, the lights were lowered and a roar rose from the Garden crowd. As I was to learn, there was nothing like that timeless moment when the houselights fell at a Dead show *anywhere*: the expectations, the hope, the excitement, the possibilities ... and the predictions ! During the jam bridging "Scarlet Begonias" to "Fire on the Mountain," the group's female vocalist transformed into a psychedelic Ella Fitzgerald, unleashing vocal scat that was both hypnotic and beautiful. My trip synchronized perfectly with the range of emotions being conveyed through her vocals.

I was pretty much sold right there.

The lead guitarist seemed to possess, and emit, other-worldly energies. He gently strummed the opening chords to a tale titled "Terrapin Station," slowly, and intentionally, building the music's momentum, completely in control of the art being created onstage — Ron Guidry with a guitar. As I would later learn, "Terrapin," like "Morning Dew," was one of the few songs that Garcia allowed himself to revel in the spotlight, let his hair down, put aside his modesty for a moment, and shred. The song exploded as he declared "Inspiration !" There was a voluminous crowd reaction. As best I could tell, the music was now being powered by the tribal pounding of the two drummers.

"Terrapin" raised the Garden roof, and Chris and I were all aboard. Only by the grace of a benevolent God were we able to come down by the time the Dead finished the hymn "Wharf Rat."

After the encore, we had exactly 20 minutes to exit the Garden, catch a cab, and board the northbound Harlem Line train out of Grand Central Station. We couldn't find a taxi, so we made the hasty decision to hop into a gypsy cab, then a common mode of transportation in the city. Driving uptown on Sixth Avenue, the driver missed the right onto E. 42nd Street and headed for pre-Rudy Giuliani Times Square.

My brother and I quickly realized the driver wasn't a gypsy cab owner but a pedophile hoping to find depravity in Times Square with two teenagers. Nothing like an ungodly imposition in your young world while tripping for the first time ! While this experience may illustrate the downside of living in the city, it also demonstrates the benefit: From the passenger side seat, I delivered a Larry Holmes-like left to the driver's jaw while Chris unloaded a Bruce Lee kick to the back of his head. The driver promptly pulled over. "You're lucky we don't have the time to beat the shit out of you," I yelled.

We jumped out of the car, hooting and hollering like two teens experiencing all the craziness of a brave new world for the first time in, of all places, Times Square. We stopped to gaze at the lights and color around us, our feet nailed to the concrete, convinced we were at the Center of the Universe.

Laughing all the way, we ran to Grand Central on legs toned by summers spent caddying, shouting with youthful glee as we jumped between the closing doors of the 11:30 p.m. northbound Con Rail with no time to spare.

As we sat down, I was certain we were both glowing, an aura that told everyone on board we were tripping on fantastic blotter. The train pulled into the 125th Street station and the routine of having made it, relatively unscathed, to the first stop grounded us. In our seats, I asked Chris, "Would you do it again ?"

"Getting in that gypsy cab ?"

"Very funny," I said. "The acid or seeing the Dead."

"I'd do both again," he said. "What about you ?"

It was my turn. "I'd definitely see them again, the acid kicked ass with the music, and the chicks were all hot."

May 1, 1941

Jerry Garcia's intellect and intriguing mind are both on display in the story behind his selection of the name Rosebud for his Doug Irwin-built guitar, which he played onstage with the Grateful Dead and the Garcia Band from 1990 until his death in 1995.

Jerry was a huge movie buff.

In several interviews, he discussed the impact film had on his life, starting with the 1948 flick, *Abbott and Costello Meet Frankenstein*. Shortly before his passing, Garcia sat down with AMC for a show titled "The Movie That Changed My Life." He talked fondly of seeing *Abbott and Costello Meet Frankenstein*: "It scared and fascinated me. I was six years old. My father had died the previous year, in '47, so that also made it a heavy time in my life, emotionally. A big reason for my clamping onto it ... [was] the thing of a dead thing brought to life."

The duality of the Dracula character also intrigued Jerry, leading him to make this observation: "There's a powerful consciousness and there's a weak consciousness and one of them is going to dominate the other."

He also revealed the Abbott and Costello film introduced him to other types of cinema. "The iconography ... the Frankenstein monster, Dracula and the Wolfman became figures of tremendous fascination for me. Overwhelming. It led me to, for example, the discovery of things like German Expressionist theatre and film [and] the James Whale original *Frankenstein* (1931). These things are all personal icons in my life. They have tremendous power."

SET ONE

Citizen Kane, widely-regarded as the greatest film of all time, was one of the late guitarist's favorite movies. Released on May 1, 1941, *Citizen Kane* was directed and produced by Orson Welles, who also stars in the classic as newspaper magnate Charles Foster Kane, a character loosely based on the life of publisher William Randolph Hearst.

The story is told through flashbacks, with a newspaper reporter attempting to resolve the mystery of why Kane's dying word was "Rosebud."

The 1965 film, *The Saragossa Manuscript*, a noir classic from the Polish School of mid-'60s cinema directed by Wojciech Has, was another of Garcia's favorite films. In the 1990s, Jerry, along with Martin Scorsese and Francis Ford Coppola, put up much of the money needed to restore *The Saragossa Manuscript*.

Sadly, Garcia did not live long enough to see the project come to fruition in 2001.

What drew Jerry to *Citizen Kane* and *The Saragossa Manuscript* ?

The plots in both movies unfold in highly-unconventional ways: *Citizen Kane* uses flashback sequences while *The Saragossa Manuscript*, writes one film critic, is "a tale-within-a-tale-within-a-tale, [which] only begins to describe [its] complexity, because some of the inner tales intertwine."

In *Citizen Kane*, a bed-ridden Charles Foster Kane lies near death, a snow globe in hand. As he utters the word "Rosebud" with his dying breath, the snow globe slips from his grasp and shatters on the floor. A newspaper reporter sets out to uncover the mystery of "Rosebud."

The scribe discovers that, as a child, Kane grew up poor but happy in his parents' Colorado boarding house. At age eight, a gold mine was discovered on his family's property, and his mother decided to send the boy off to live with a wealthy banker named Walter Parks Thatcher so the child could receive an education.

Kane is happily playing with a sled in the snow when he's told by his mother that he's being sent away to live with Thatcher; the boy protests vehemently but to no avail. The sleigh is then ripped from his hands by the cold-hearted banker.

Under Thatcher's tutelage, Charles Foster Kane goes on to live a disingenuous life as a newspaper publisher who makes his fortune through yellow journalism, preying on people's fears to bolster circulation. The stock market crash of 1929 forces Kane to sell the controlling interest in his newspaper empire to Thatcher, a devastating move for the magnate, given his deep resentment of the banker.

Kane attempts to rebuild his life by marrying a daughter of the U.S. president and entering the political arena, embarking on a run for governor of New York that ends in humiliation when it's discovered he's having an affair. He divorces and remarries but continues to live an unfulfilled, and troubled, life.

As the movie nears its conclusion, Kane spies the old snow globe, a source of solitude for him, as the "snow" evokes memories of his childhood and the sled, when life was simple and good. The film ends with Thatcher's staff going through his personal belongings, deciding which items to keep and which to discard. The camera pans to Kane's childhood sled, which is then tossed into a burning pile inside a blazing furnace.

Its brand name ?

Rosebud.

"Rosebud was the thing that [Kane] most wanted but couldn't seem to have," observes luthier Doug Irwin, who crafted five guitars for Garcia. In a 2009 interview with dozin.com, he said, "When I finished [the] guitar for [Jerry] — the one that became Rosebud, it has the skeleton saint on it, [a] skeleton saint in the act of repelling death — [Jerry] said, 'Well, what's the name of it ?' and I said, 'Listen, I just did the inlay, you got to come up with the name.'

"I thought it was really interesting that Jerry picked that name [Rosebud] for the guitar."

What did the name signify to both Garcia and Charles Foster Kane ?

Childhood being clutched from their hands.

For Kane, that moment arrived when the sled was wrestled from his grasp by Thatcher. For Jerry, it came as a five-year-old, when his dad's life was snatched from him right before his eyes. (Joe Garcia slipped on a rock while fly fishing with Jerry and his older brother, Tiff, in the Trinity River, plunged into the deep rapids, and drowned.)

A small but insightful look into Jerry's mind.

October 16, 1947

Bob occasionally played a beat-up Fender Telecaster onstage from 2003 to 2007.

The guitar's story begins on October 16, 1947, when Bobby was born and given up for adoption by his biological parents. His mother, a single college student from Tucson, AZ, and his biological father, also a Tucson student, briefly relocated to the Bay Area, where the couple had their child and arranged for the baby's adoption.

In the late 1980s, the mother, who had returned to Tucson after the birth, reached out to Bob, identifying herself by giving the fake name she had used on Weir's birth certificate. She then told Bob his biological father's name — John Parber, making Bobby's "birth name" Robert Parber.

John Parber forged a career in the Air Force, rising to colonel, a rank that placed him in charge of the Hamilton Air Force Base in Marin County. In the early 1990s, Bobby hired a detective to track down Mr. Parber but, upon learning he was military, decided not to pursue the issue. "I'm pathologically anti-authoritarian," he explained to SFGate.com in a 2004 interview.

In 1996, Bob's wife, Natascha, convinced him to reach out to Parber. "I'm Robert Weir of Mill Valley," began the first phone call.

"The only Robert Weir I know plays guitar for the Grateful Dead," the colonel answered.

Bobby, Natascha, John Parber and Parber's wife hit if off instantly, with the Parbers becoming, in Bob's words, "doting grandparents" to Weir's then-infant daughters. In the early 2000s, Bobby would often visit the Parbers and occasionally spend the night in a spare bedroom, where he noticed a beat-up Fender Telecaster, its strings broken and pickup snapped.

The Parbers had raised four children and one, James Louis Parber, was a musician who had played guitar in the local group Lawrence Hammond and the Whiplash Band as well as in a Billy C. Farlow (Commander Cody) solo band. After a 12-year battle, James Parber passed away from spinal cancer in 1991.

Bobby fell in love with the Telecaster but also knew James' three siblings had left the guitar with their parents as a keepsake and reminder of their brother. He respectfully asked the Parbers if he could restore it. They happily obliged.

Weir first used the guitar onstage during Dead tours in 2003 and 2004. "The Telecaster has a thin, reedy sound," Bob told SFGate.com. "[It] made the band sound jell. It was instantly perfect. It cleared out a lot of clutter."

A little research by Bobby revealed the guitar is a vintage 1956 Fender Telecaster, one of Fender's original models.

Playing James Louis Parber's six-string was Bob's way of honoring his late half-brother, the Parber family, and John Parber, who passed away in 2015.

1959

Could the 1959 suspense novel *The Manchurian Candidate* by Richard Condon be the source from which Robert Hunter drew inspiration for the lyric "I can tell the Queen of Diamonds by the way she shine" in "Loser," the bleak gambling tale on Jerry's first solo album, *Garcia* ?

The film version of *The Manchurian Candidate* was released on October 24, 1962 — at the height of the Cuban Missile Crisis. The movie was well received, nominated for two Academy Awards and later chosen for preservation in the National Film Archive by the Library of Congress.

In the film, three-time Academy Award-nominated actress Angela Lansbury plays Eleanor Iselin, the wife of a powerful American senator and a KGB operative who uses the Queen of Diamonds playing card to control her son, Raymond Shaw, a staff sergeant in the Korean War who was among a platoon of soldiers taken prisoner and brainwashed.

After being kidnapped in Korea, Shaw, played by Laurence Harvey, and his platoon are transported to Manchuria, China, where the soldiers are conditioned to believe Shaw is a hero who rescued the troop. Shaw is brainwashed to act as a cold-blooded assassin who follows the next command given to him — with no memory afterward — upon being shown an image of the Queen of Diamonds.

Hunter's experiences as a participant in the government-sponsored LSD experiments at Stanford Hospital in 1959 exposed him to mind-control and brain-washing techniques; the use of the term "Queen of Diamonds" in "Loser" seems to connect his experiences at Stanford to *The Manchurian Candidate*.

But unless the Grateful Dead's bard speaks, we may never know for certain.

Explains Garcia, "We made an effort … to leave [our lyrics] ambiguous on purpose. I always like songs that hint at either a larger story or something slightly more mysterious, so we make the lyrics as obscure as possible. Our fans desire some mystery."

According to writer David Willis McCullough, Senator Johnny Iselin was based on Republican senator Joseph McCarthy, while Condon admitted he modeled Eleanor Iselin after Roy Cohn, McCarthy's despicable chief counsel during the pair's inquisition into Communist activities in America during the 1950s.

Ms. Lansbury's role as Iselin is widely-regarded as her finest acting moment. Frank Sinatra also starred in *The Manchurian Candidate*, playing Major Bennett Marco, who was among the soldiers captured and brainwashed. After meeting another member of the troop who's experiencing the same recurring nightmare, Marco contacts Shaw to get to the root of what really happened in Manchuria.

Robert Hunter has no problem remembering what happened at Stanford Hospital: "The government was interested in seeing what LSD did to my audiometer responses. They wanted to see if I was more hypnotic, or if I could be hypnotized more easily, on a drug than without it. This guy came in and started running audiometer tests. I was sitting in [a] chair and he was running these tests. He'd come in, draw 5 cc's of blood every two hours or so, and then run these tests on me."

1962

Ken Kesey also took part in the LSD experiments at Stanford Hospital while enrolled in the Creative Writing Program at Stanford University, where he was both a Woodrow Wilson fellow and a Saxton Prize recipient. The then-aspiring author recalled his own experiences at the hospital: "There were about 120 of us, students and non-students. The government wanted somebody to look into 'that room.' They said, 'Hey, we got a great room, we discovered this nice room. Let's get somebody to go in there and look it over.' When I walked out, they said, 'Don't let anybody else know.'"

Like Hunter, the Stanford experiments would go on to inform Kesey's writing.

However, the title of his first novel, *One Flew Over the Cuckoo's Nest* (1962), came from a different source — a line in a nursery rhyme recited to him by his grandmother:

Vintery, mintery, cutery, corn,
Apple seed and apple thorn,
Wire, briar, limber lock
Three geese in a flock
One flew East

One flew West
And one flew over the cuckoo's nest

Merry Prankster and renowned mime Joe McCord was living at Kesey's house in La Honda as the novelist finished his book. "I was an insomniac," recalls Joe. "I used to listen to him tell me about how terrible the conditions were ... horrific stories. I would just let him talk, and I would listen. Then he'd go to the small house out back (where Kesey finished *Cuckoo's Nest*) and start typing."

In 2005, *Time* included *One Flew Over the Cuckoo's Nest* on its list of the "100 Best English-Language Novels from 1923 to 2005."

The film version of *Cuckoo's Nest* was ranked No. 33 on the American Film Institute's "100 Years ... 100 Movies" list in 2015.

"Ken wasn't involved with the film," notes Mr. McCord. "He wanted the story to be told through the eyes of the Chief, but Miloš Forman insisted it be told from McMurphy's perspective. Ken believed, as I do, that it would have been a much more interesting film and a better film."

Despite Kesey's lack of involvement, *Cuckoo's Nest* became one of only three films (the other two are 1934's *It Happened One Night* and 1991's *The Silence of the Lambs*) to capture the Academy Awards' "Big Five," including Best Picture, Best Actor (Jack Nicholson) and Best Actress (Louise Fletcher).

1963

Bobby went back to the impetuous days of his youth to find a muse for his critically-acclaimed 2016 album, *Blue Mountain*. "I thought it would be a terribly romantic thing to run away and be a cowboy, which I did," Weir told "CBS This Morning: Saturday."

"You were 15 when you did this?" asked show anchor Anthony Mason.

"Yeah," said Weir of his 1963 jaunt to Big Sky country.

Three years earlier, Phil Lesh had sought out the same adventure, attempting to hitchhike to Calgary in the summer of 1960 to work in the oilfields. "I got as far as Spokane," Lesh told author David Gans. "My buddy, whose uncle in Spokane was supposed to have connections in the oilfields, didn't. That led to one of the great experiences in my life, which was riding the rails. A boxcar, from Spokane to Seattle. What an experience ! I remember sneaking on early in the morning. It took only 36 hours !"

Life as a ranch hand, Bobby soon found out, wasn't all that it was cracked up to be. He would later describe the experience as a "bait-and-switch," laughing at his naïveté.

"I found my way out to Wyoming and got to work on a ranch out there," he told Mason. "And I was, you know, living in a bunk house. I was the kid on the ranch, so I got to shovel a lot of stalls."

Despite the shitty job, the songs that became *Blue Mountain* took root during long, starry nights on the wide-open Wyoming range. "There wasn't much to do but tell stories and sing songs. And that's what we did. I was the kid with the guitar. I won't say I learned those songs, but halfway learned them. And I've been packing that around with me for years, that whole aesthetic."

Which prompts Mason to ask, "And how would you describe that aesthetic ?"

"High, wide and lonesome," answers Bobby, as if summarizing the tenor of *Blue Mountain*.

December 4, 1965

At the San Jose Acid Test, the Grateful Dead performed under their new name for the first time, having just changed their moniker from the Warlocks. They had become aware of at least two other groups, including a band in Florida, using the same tag. "We were trying to think up names and for about two or three weeks we went on the usual thing of, like, coming up with thousands and thousands of very funny names but none of which we could use," recalled Jerry. "Like the Vivisectionists ..."

"... and the Reality Sandwich," kicks in Weir.

During a band get-together at Phil's place in Palo Alto, Garcia randomly opened a dictionary and, as fate decreed, Grateful Dead leapt off the page. "It just ... canceled my mind out," stated Jerry. "I thought, 'Well, you know ...' So, we, we decided to have it, but it was funny 'cause we didn't really like it too much at first, and we thought it was ... it kinda made us shudder. And, uh, you know we were worried: 'Aw, nobody's gonna go for it — it's too weird.' But, finally, enough people called us that and we called ourselves that enough times that that's who we [became]."

Very little is known about the evening of December 4, 1965, as no setlists, recordings or photographs exist. "We were all living on Waverley Street in Palo Alto," remembers Hunter. "The crew just picked up Jerry and split."

The gig was held in a home referred to as "Big Nig's House." One can assume people were tripping on Owsley's acid, including the band, save for Pigpen. The Dead, led by Mr. McKernan, likely served up lengthy takes on "Viola Lee Blues" and "Good Morning, Little Schoolgirl," inciting the debauchery and madness being perpetuated around them by Kesey, Neal Cassady and the Merry Pranksters.

A few weeks after Garcia's death in 1995, the remaining members of the Dead wisely elected to call it a day and not dilute their legacy, forever retiring the name Grateful Dead, according to a band press release, "out of our love and respect for what we created together."

Despite concert promoter Peter Shapiro's best efforts to pimp out the name "Grateful Dead" in the summer of 2015, the band did not reunite for their 50th anniversary shows in Santa Clara and Chicago using the name Grateful Dead.

Of the Dead's legendary, and apropos, name, Mr. Hunter once observed, "In the end, a name will shape what you become.

1966

Sometime in 1966, four of the five members of an infant Grateful Dead (Phil was absent) sat down with an unnamed Bay Area disc jockey on an unknown radio station for an in-depth interview that covers the key transitional period in the Dead's history of 1965-66, when the band put aside any pop aspirations and delved deeply into psychedelia.

DJ: Our perspective tonight — we want to lead off the whole thing by talking to some wild characters called the Grateful Dead. I should have had you guys on before because you're one of the popular groups around the area. I've had other groups and I said "OK, who's sounding good ?" And they said, "The Grateful Dead." And I just finally got around to getting you on the show. Around the, uh, table we'll go, meet first Pigpen. What a horrible name.

Pigpen: Not my fault, Jerry gave it to me.

DJ: What's your real name ?

Pigpen: Ron.

DJ: Ron ? Uh, your fan club yesterday or something was telling me you're 21 years old ...

Pigpen: Um-hm.

DJ: You look like 38 ... what happened ?

Pigpen: Umm ... couldn't tell ya.

DJ: Uh, Jerry Garcia. Jerry was on a previous show with us when Ken Kesey was down. And Jerry's name is mentioned quite often when we talk about guitar pickers. Many times on this show ...

Garcia: Guitar pickers ...

DJ: Yeah, we've talked about guitar and who's doing this well and that well and somebody always mentions Jerry Garcia. It's good to have you back on the show.

Garcia: Thanks.

DJ: And a wild shirt on today. Uh, Bob was the real name ... I didn't catch ... Bill, oh, first of all, Bill ... OK, doesn't matter.

Kreutzmann: Uh, Bill Kreutzmann's the real name ...

DJ: Kreutzmann ...

SET ONE

Kreutzmann: ... it's just too long to pronounce.

DJ: And your instrument is ...

Kreutzmann: Drums.

DJ: Drums. OK, and Bob ...

Weir: I'm the rhythm guitarist.

DJ: Are you the spokesman for the group ? You threw something like an 18-syllable word out a while ago here ... knocked the whole thing dead. Is he the mouthpiece ?

Garcia: No, that was a long mumble.

DJ: Oh, is that what it was ? And there's one member ... better give him credit.

Garcia: Phil Lesh ... who's the bass player, who's off on an errand or something ... somewhere.

DJ: And, well, off on an errand is fine ... yeah. But the Grateful Dead, playing almost every weekend somewhere or another around San Francisco ... things have been going pretty good for you, right ?

Garcia: Oh yeah, I'd say so.

Weir: Real good.

Garcia: Remarkably good.

DJ: I've had a chance to catch you a couple, three times at the Fillmore ... a lot of good blues. And, uh, one thing I know about the Dead, seems like the instruments ... everything is always right together, there's never any sloppiness ... *bing-bang*, you know, the guitars are always ... everybody hits at the right time. Is that what it is ?

Garcia: It's pure luck.

DJ: OK, where did the name "Grateful Dead" come from, and how did the group get organized ?

Pigpen (to Garcia): Run it down to him.

Garcia: OK, we were, uh, we were trying to think of a name for the band. Our name was originally the Warlocks, not "Originally the Warlocks," just "the Warlocks." But first it was ... anyway ... the Warlocks was our new name now. We discovered that there was a band back east, or something like that, recording under that name. We decided ... oh, no, we can't have that, we can't be confused with somebody else.

DJ: That's a wild thing ... the names of groups. Somebody just came up with the "Grateful Dead" and it sounded right ?

Garcia: Well, no, we didn't come up with it. Here's what happened. We were standing around in utter desperation at Phil's house and there was a huge Webster's New World Dictionary, I believe. Big, ya know ? A big monolithic thing. And I just opened it up. And there in huge black letters was "The Grateful Dead" and it was just so ... *ya know ?*

Kreutzmann: Prophesied out of the book.

DJ: About a year you've been together then ?

Garcia: Uh, year-and-a-half ... just about a year-and-a-half.

DJ (to Kreutzmann): Bill, how'd the group get together ... what were all of you doing ?

Kreutzmann: We were working separately at other jobs as musicians — other bands.

Weir: Jerry, me and Pigpen were in a jugband — Mother McCree's Uptown Jug Champions.

Kreutzmann: We had a different bass player {Dana Morgan, Jr.} at one time, who brought us all together and knew all of us. We didn't really know each other necessarily, and [he] put us all together.

DJ: And then he canceled the scene, huh ?

Kreutzmann: Yeah, he couldn't ... he couldn't play six nights at the clubs and things, so we found another bass player.

DJ: How often do you have to rehearse ? Or do you rehearse ?

Garcia: We try to rehearse every day, and, um, we put in about six hours a day.

DJ: Really ?

Garcia: Yeah, well, that's because it's the only thing we do, really.

DJ: Yeah.

Garcia: We try and do it as good as we can and put as much time as we can in on it, but because we're all human beings and we're all friends, we can't make it work, you know, I mean we can't be ... we can't say, "OK, this is punch in and let's play and then punch out." It's like we get together and sometimes we might not play at all, we might just sit around talking for an hour or so, telling jokes or something, and then play a little and get some ideas and it kinda works like that.

DJ: Oh. Pigpen, you, uh, play sitting down — all the time ?

Pigpen: Not any more.

DJ (perplexed): Not anymore ?

SET ONE

Garcia: Pig buried the stool.

DJ: That kinda canceled out my question, didn't it. I was gonna ... all right, why did you play sitting ?

Pigpen: It was to easier to play that way.

DJ: Is that right ? Just, uh, straight guitar, though, I mean, you like sitting down doing it ?

Pigpen: Not any more.

DJ: I thought maybe you were an Arthur Lyman reject or something, with the old Hawaiian guitar.

Garcia: Well, he plays the organ ... organ and harmonica. He's not one of the guitar players. He, uh ...

Pigpen (to Jerry): Thanks for straightening it out.

Garcia: OK, don't mention it ... anytime (laughing). And, uh, the thing about the organ is that ...

Pigpen (interjecting): ... you're stuck to it.

Garcia: ... you have this foot pedal, you know, and it's more comfortable for Pigpen to sit down and work the foot pedal, but we've ... after a few ...

Pigpen (interjecting): ... prodded me (laughing).

Garcia: ... sessions of, uh ... (laughing).

Pigpen: ... long sticks (laughing).

Garcia: ... we finally convinced him.

Pigpen: ... then they threw my seat away.

DJ: Yeah, I hear there's something called the "Pigpen T-shirt."

Pigpen: Yeah.

DJ: Does that mean you've arrived ... you're a star now or something ?

Pigpen: Well, it's their fault ... over there, sitting down.

DJ: They're the fan club sitting down in the other part of the room.

Pigpen: Yep.

DJ: I'll have to get a hold of one of them. Are they in production right now or something ?

Pigpen: The people wanted to do it for you.

DJ: Oh, is that for me ?

Pigpen: That's for you.

DJ: All right !

Weir: Good news ... it's fluorescent, no less.

DJ: Oh, is that lovely. Yes, it is you. And I remember the picture now of one of the posters that, I think, Family Dog did. Didn't he use the same picture ? Or somebody ?

Garcia: Who knows ?

DJ: I don't know, they're so many posters. Lovely things, too. Hey, thank you. I'll figure out somewhere to wear that (laughter).

Garcia: Wear it anywhere.

August 28, 1967

On a sunny Monday afternoon, August 28, 1967, the Grateful Dead performed in the Lindley Meadows section of Golden Gate Park in honor of Chocolate George, a 35-year-old member of the Hells Angels killed four days earlier in a collision with a car on Haight Street. His funeral, held earlier in the day, included an honor guard of more than 200 Angels.

According to Diggers.org, Chocolate George was "really liked ... for his Cossack general's appearance, his Russian fur hat, and his overall fearless, friendly attitude toward everyone, except would-be tough guys or bullies, whom he crushed."

The biker, whose real name was Charles George Hendricks, got his nickname from his love of chocolate milk, which he was always drinking. (He was buried with two quarts inside his coffin.)

Chocolate George's bike was clipped by a carful of sight-seers, a final reminder that the so-called Summer of Love in 1967 was neither groovy nor a manifestation of an incipient ideology. "It got really strange when the [Gray Line tour] buses started coming by [in the spring of 1967]," Garcia would later tell *Rolling Stone*. "Until then, somehow everything seemed possible on every level. Any possibility for it being a community on a communicative level was shot. Pretty soon, the cops were everywhere."

If there were an actual "Summer of Love," one that was both groovy and filled with heady idealism, it had already come and gone. Kick-started by the Acid Tests in December, 1965, it was brought to a triumphant climax at the Great Human Be-In in the Polo Field on January 14, 1967.

On October 6, six weeks after George's passing, the Diggers held a "Death of the Hippie and Birth of the

Free Man" ceremony. A cardboard coffin filled with trinkets, knickknacks and other artifacts from the Haight was symbolically cremated. "That was all of us saying, 'We're not gonna tell anybody anymore,'" commented Garcia.

Chocolate George's favorite band — the Grateful Dead — and Big Brother and the Holding Company each played sets in front of a crowd of 1,000 people on August 28. "George loved Be-Ins and happenings," explained his best friend, Hairy Henry Kot. "So, we thought we'd have a happening just for him."

February 14, 1968

1968 was a pivotal year for the Grateful Dead, marked by musical exploration and rapid evolution. They became a deeply psychedelic band, immersing themselves onstage in the psychotomimetic sounds and textures featured on *Anthem of the Sun*.

During the first half of '68, the Carousel Ballroom became the Dead's primary base of operations, as the intimacy of its room allowed them to refine their improvisational approach to live performance.

Originally a Swing Era ballroom, the Carousel was still in its pristine state — right down to the original chandeliers and lush carpeting — when it was purchased by the Grateful Dead and the Jefferson Airplane from the Irish League of San Francisco. After the two bands added a stage, there was enough room for 2,500 people, enabling fans to watch the Dead's musical transformation front-row-and-center.

The Carousel opened on Valentine's Day, 1968, with Country Joe and the Fish warming up for the Dead, who were mourning the recent death of Cassady. Before the start of their second set, Jerry said: "We respectfully dedicate this set to Neal Cassady."

The set began with "Cryptical Envelopment", "The Other One," a powerful tribute to Cowboy Neal. The band got trippy next, with "New Potato Caboose", "Born Cross-Eyed" (which is how the two songs are paired on *Anthem of the Sun*) and a zesty, nine-minute "Spanish Jam." From here, trusty front man Pigpen grabbed the reigns, taking everyone home with "Alligator", "Caution", "In the Midnight Hour."

During the weekend of March 15-17, 1968, the Dead played a three-night stand at the Carousel. After one of the first two gigs, Jerry was infuriated. "I'd come off the stage, boy, sometimes really, really upset, you know ? And when I was younger, I would get even more upset, I'd get more crazy, I would want it to be really good.

"And I would think, 'Wow, it's not where I want it [to] be. It's almost there, but it's not there.'

"Then I'd get really angry. I remember [the night in March, 1968 when] we did the Carousel, and we recorded. I got really upset at the end of the set. I thought it was just horrible, for some reason. It seemed like everything was a struggle.

"I got real pissed off at Phil and grabbed him and threw him down this little flight of stairs. It was like, 'Man, I've never done that.' And Phil, I've been really tight with him for years.

"I was that freaked out, and high, too. Flipped out, man. The music was fucking [with me]."

Phil recalled the moment in his biography, *Searching for the Sound*: "At one point in the show, I entered a state of total brain-sag — frighteningly, nothing that was being played made any *sense* to me … I was so panicked that I stopped playing. I suddenly noticed that Jerry was *glaring* at me … I stared blankly back at him.

"After the show … I encountered Jerry at the top of the stairs leading to the dressing room. He grabbed me by the collar, and snarled, 'You play, motherfucker !' and shoved me aside. I tripped over my own feet and fell down the stairs right on my ass. Jerry was normally such a sweetheart that I was shocked beyond belief.

"At the gig the following evening, Jerry was apologetic: 'Sorry, man — I don't know what came over me.'"

"We listened to these tapes months later and ended up using them on our album [*Anthem*]," noted Garcia. "They were crackling with energy, they were amazing."

Lesh agreed: "The show was spectacular, teeming brilliantly with ideas and contrasts."

"That's when I knew, 'Well, fuck, I've just got to keep my mouth shut and just not even think about whether it seemed like it was happening to me or not,'" concluded Jerry.

Despite their experiences as the house band for the Acid Tests, the Grateful Dead were still relatively wide-eyed and innocent as 1968 began. Jerry had not yet been burdened with the albatross of iconic stature; he was, simply, the guitar player in Pigpen's band. Bobby and Phil were learning the ropes and trying to harness the power, and Mickey and Billy were just months into a life-long partnership.

May 2, 1970

Phil was asked when he first realized the Grateful Dead's music had "infinite possibilities."

"It was the first time we stretched out 'Viola Lee Blues,'" he told *Rolling Stone*. "We worked up into this frenzy and, without a count, we came slamming back down into the groove and finished the song. I somewhat ingenuously turned to Jerry and said, '*Man, this could be art !*'"

"All of us have a sense of time that's funny at best," observed Jerry. "We've learned to keep it the same type of funny."

"Viola Lee Blues" was the Dead's most raucous live song during the period 1966-70.

Yet, six months after the Grateful Dead's earth-shattering performance of "Viola Lee Blues" at Harpur College in Binghamton, NY on May 2, 1970 (easily one of the band's finest shows), the Dead stopped performing the Noah Lewis-penned prison tale. The song's final appearance came out on the east end of Long Island at SUNY-Stony Brook during the early show on Halloween night 1970.

Why would the Grateful Dead stop playing their most exciting live song ?

Garcia asked the band to discontinue "Viola Lee," as he felt they could no longer effortlessly bring the song around to "the drop," that cataclysmic moment when the cacophony of the jam coalesces back into the song's rhythmic, walking blues. "Jerry didn't want to do 'Viola Lee' after a certain point, because we had lost the ability to bring it back down like that," notes Phil.

The quintessential "Viola Lee Blues" took place on April 26, 1969 in Chicago, the version selected by Phil for the *Fallout From the Phil Zone* album. The song's seismic drop at the 17:53 mark exemplifies how the Grateful Dead were able to, in Mr. Lesh's words, "[come] slamming back down into the groove."

When the Dead successfully pulled off "Viola Lee," it was a head-on collision between raw power and intuitive musicianship. "It [was] one of those wonderful things, [but the second] you start thinking about it, it won't happen," says Phil. "And that is what happened."

May 3, 1970

"GRATEFUL DEAD CONCERT IS FREE AND OPEN-AIR"

Wesleyan Argus

May 1, 1970

Crowd estimates from various sources ranging from 10,000 to 30,000 have been projected for Sunday's free, open-air concert of the Grateful Dead [on May 3].

By transferring funds from several committees to the social committee, the College Body Committee has been able to raise the necessary money for the concert to go on as scheduled.

The CBC also pledged a total of $2,500 against next fall's revenues from the College Body Tax. In addition, individual students have signed pledges totaling over $3,000 for "contingency damages," should the need arise.

Also appearing at Sunday's concert will be seven or eight other bands provided through the efforts of the Better Days Prospecting Company, a traveling commune that will be seeking recruits. In addition, Gary Michaels of Better Days states that there is a good possibility that members of the cast of *Hair*, plus people from the Hog Farm commune, will be coming up for the affair.

Bands appearing will be Randy Burns and the Morning After (from New Haven), Bone (New Haven), Joy (New Haven), Nighthawks (Middletown), Trod Tiger and the Tunafish (New Haven), and, tentatively, Charisma (New Britain).

Security for the potentially massive affair is being provided by student marshals. All those wishing to be marshals should report to the bandstand on Andrus field by noon Sunday. Additional regular Wesleyan security guards will also be posted at dormitories.

Facilities for a first aid center are also being planned for the concert in the area of Nicholson Lounge.

General information and job lists for those interested in helping out with other organizational aspects of the concert will be available at a table especially set up for that purpose at Downey House. Questions may also be addressed to Dave White, Tom Morse, or Kathy Fitzgerald.

West College is also attempting to supply free food for the crowd at the concert. Donations to buy food may be sent to Box 218, addressed to "Free Food."

"Student responsibility will be the key to the success of the Grateful Dead concert this Sunday," said David White '70, speaking at an organizational meeting in Howland Lounge Thursday night.

In the event of rain, the concert will be held in the Cage, but will be then open only to Wesleyan students and one guest.

(*The Argus* also warns concert attendees about the university code policies on "the unauthorized use of fireworks, the turning in of false fire alarms, the use of alcohol ... [and] the possession and/ or use of drugs.")

May 6, 1970

As part of a nation-wide campus movement protesting the shooting deaths of four students by the Ohio Army National Guard at Kent State University on May 4, 1970, the Grateful Dead performed a free show on May 6 in Kresge Plaza on the campus of the Massachusetts Institute of Technology in Cambridge.

At MIT, the Dead's nine-song set began with "Dancing in the Streets," bringing some respite from the traumatic events of May 4 to the student-dominated audience. A segue of "China Cat Sunflower", "I Know You, Rider" followed, before Pigpen sang "Next Time You See Me." Garcia led the band through a stinging, eleven-minute "Morning Dew" that gave voice to the unrest and anger blanketing the campus. His closing solo is lengthy and protracted, especially for 1970, and Phil's counterpoint sublime.

After a rollicking "Not Fade Away," with Pigpen starring on background vocals, Bobby declares, "We're gonna split and we'll be playing for you tomorrow night but it's just too fucking cold. You know how it is."

Jerry adds, "Bye, now. It's a pleasure playing for y'all."

The tragedy at Kent State magnified the atrocities of an unjustifiable war in Vietnam, the difficulties faced by Americans gathering peacefully to protest, and the unchecked brutality by the police and armed services during demonstrations and protests.

Throughout their career, the Grateful Dead clearly demonstrated both a strong political bent and sensibility, performing shows in support of groups, individuals and causes such as the Mime Troupe; the Black Panthers; the Columbia University students arrested for protesting on their campus in May, 1968; the homeless; AIDS awareness programs, and environmental issues, to name a few.

Buoyed by the Dead's performance, many of the young people gathered in Kresge Plaza on May 6 could begin the process of healing.

For a wounded nation, its psyche already scarred by the ongoing Vietnam War and the recent assassinations of Martin Luther King and Bobby Kennedy, the Kent State shootings served as another sobering mandate for immediate social and political change in America.

July, 1970

From Phil going on a dinner date with photographer Linda Eastman (later McCartney) to Paul inviting Bobby to sit in with him in Boston during the summer of 2016, Deadheads are always searching for stories connecting the Grateful Dead to the Beatles.

Well, here's a really cool tale !

During one of the two Calgary shows on the Festival Express tour, the Grateful Dead's five-date journey across Canada aboard a chartered Canadian National Railways train in June and July, 1970, Jerry and Delaney Bramlett joined Ian and Sylvia and their band onstage for "C.C. Rider."

For the guest spot, Garcia played a 1968 Rosewood Fender Telecaster (serial #235594) originally owned by none other than George Harrison, who used the same exact six-string to record the *Let It Be* album in January, 1969, play the Beatles' historic 42-minute roof-top gig atop Apple Corps on January 30, 1969 (their last public performance), and record "Badge" with Cream.

Dhani Harrison, George's son, declared it was his dad's favorite guitar.

Fender gave the custom-made solid Rosewood Telecaster, crafted by Fender luthier Phil Kubicki, to George in December, 1968.

The website FeelNumb.com adds, "On December 1, 1969, Harrison attended a performance by Delaney & Bonnie at London's Royal Albert Hall. Eric Clapton was on the bill that night and following the show asked Harrison if he would join the group for a few shows throughout Britain and Denmark. The next day, Harrison joined the tour and presented Delaney Bramlett with the guitar."

Harrison said to Bramlett, "This is for what you did for me last night."

Delaney & Bonnie were one of the opening bands on the Festival Express tour; Delaney Bramlett loaned the Rosewood Telecaster to Garcia at one of the Calgary shows on July 4 and 5, when the pair joined Ian and Sylvia and the Great Speckled Bird for "C.C. Rider."

Billy, in a cowboy hat, also got in on the fun, keeping time on a tambourine as Jerry wailed on George's Telecaster !

In addition to Ian and Sylvia, the Festival Express bill also featured (among other acts): Traffic (only in Toronto), the Band, the New Riders of the Purple Sage, Ten Years After, Mountain, the Flying Burrito Brothers, Delaney & Bonnie & Friends, Buddy Guy and headliners Janis Joplin and Full Tilt Boogie.

In 2003, Delaney Bramlett put the Rosewood Telecaster up for auction. Actor Ed Begley, Jr. bid on behalf of Olivia Harrison (George's wife) and the Harrison estate; their winning bid was $470,000.

It's curious to note that rosewood — used in the body of the Harrison Telecaster — was also used by Florida luthier Stephen Cripe to build the guitar Lightning Bolt, which Jerry played onstage with the Grateful Dead during 1993-95. Lightning Bolt would become one of Garcia's favorite guitars; Cripe used Brazilian rosewood for the fingerboard and East Indian rosewood to craft the body.

Pre-supposing that Jerry knew the history of the Rosewood Telecaster, is it wishful thinking to imagine him, alone in the middle of the night inside a boxcar as the train speeds through Saskatchewan country, ripping up Harrison's riffs on *Let It Be* classics such as "One After 909" and "For You Blue" ?

Not at all.

July 14, 1970

Famed pantomime Joseph Lennon McCord is the only person who can say he was a member of both the Merry Pranksters and the Mime Troupe, which is akin to saying you've won world championship rings as a player with the New York Yankees and Boston Celtics.

It's that remarkable.

Joe — "Merlin" in Tom Wolfe's novel, *The Electric Kool-Aid Acid Test* — studied under the French actor, director and mime Jean-Louis Barrault. Mr. McCord achieved a career zenith in 1973 when he was summoned to Geneva to perform for a then 84-year-old Charlie Chaplin, who was living in exile in Vevey, Switzerland.

A year earlier, a chance meeting with Academy Award-winning actor Walter Matthau in a Mill Valley parking lot turned into a two-hour conversation that began a close friendship between Joe and Mr. Matthau, who set up the audience with Chaplin.

Joe was kept holed up in a Geneva hotel for six days before Chaplin was ready to see him. After being brought to a dark, curtain-drawn room, from the shadows, and without turning his head, Chaplin pointed to a tiny stage and commanded: "*Exécuter.*"

Perform.

Mr. McCord's one-hour audience with "the Tramp" turned into twelve hours of performances and stories. Chaplin confided to Joe that he foresaw the rise of Hitler and Nazism as early as 1931; during a visit to Berlin that year, Chaplin had been mobbed by fans, which angered the Nazis, who later produced the 1934 propaganda book, *The Jews Are Looking at You*, to demean Chaplin. His experience in Berlin prompted Chaplin to write his masterwork, the 1940 film *The Great Dictator*, which satirized Hitler and ridiculed anti-Semitism, making it the remarkable vision of a genius mind.

Upon learning he was born on the same day — April 20, 1889 — *and at the same time* as Hitler, Chaplin told Joe that, fearing an anti-Semitic backlash, he began to list his birthday as April 16, 1889, the date recorded by history.

As Joe came off the stage after opening for Lenny Bruce one night, he was pulled aside by Bruce, who admonished him, telling Joe point-blank: "You're good, but if you want to be great, you need to learn to see the world through my eyes."

Joe's work became overtly political and bitingly satirical, which is what Bruce was suggesting, and it wasn't long before the CIA started sifting through his garbage.

Joe and Sandy Lehmann Haupt were the two youngest Pranksters among the dozen or so aboard Further, driven by Neal Cassady and captained by Kesey and Ken Babbs, when it departed La Honda on June 17 for its 1964 cross-country voyage to Manhattan. McCord "got off the bus" long before its arrival in New York, decamping in Phoenix because "there was nowhere to sleep !"

Joe and Neal were dear friends, two of a kind from the moment they met. They often tripped together; 1,000 mics of Owsley's acid was their standard dose. One night, Joe was daring enough to let Neal drive him around Northern California while they were tripping. The two Pranksters were having quite the time until a mutually-shared hallucination — a large purple dragon standing menacingly before them in the middle of the road — stopped the car (and their shenanigans) dead in its tracks.

Speaking of dear friends, Bill Graham was among Joe's closest. After he made the difficult decision to leave the Mime Troupe (which Graham was managing) over the proverbial "differences in artistic direction," Graham told Joe he would always have work for him. At the Fillmore West, McCord opened for, among other acts, the Rolling Stones, the Grateful Dead and Big Brother and the Holding Company. "I opened for the Dead many times through the years, thanks to Bill."

The Grateful Dead brought out the stars and, as their opening act, Joe got to meet them all. One night, as he was performing, he heard a rustle behind his shadow screen. When he looked behind it, there was Janis Joplin, offering him both encouragement and a belt from her bottle of Southern Comfort. Afterward, she seduced Joe, telling him, "Darling, you are coming home with me." The two carried on a torrid month-long affair; late one evening, a wired Janis arrived at Joe's place with certain physical needs and a polished brass spittoon filled to the brim with pharmaceutical cocaine. The two fucked till dawn while snorting coke. After Joe fell asleep, he was awoken by a nude Janis, standing over him, spittoon in hand, singing an a cappella "Ball and Chain" to her awe-struck lover.

Another night, Jimi Hendrix stood in the wings and watched spell-bound as Joe, on fire, tore through his skits. As he left the stage, Jimi pulled him aside and told him he was a "musician in silence." Hendrix would later kid Joe that "there wasn't too much money to be made as a mime." As if to prove many a truth is said in jest, the guitarist took a lavender jade ring off his finger and handed it to Joe, telling him to sell it if he ever needed money. Lavender jade, one of its rarest forms, has a purplish hue; the ring, Mr. Hendrix explained to Joe, had inspired him to pen "Purple Haze."

That rainy day came, and the mime sold his piece of rock-n-roll history.

On July 14, 1970, as McCord was warming up for the Grateful Dead and the New Riders of the Purple Sage at the Euphoria Ballroom in San Rafael, David Crosby stood side stage, blown away by Joe's act. Crosby, who would sit in with the Dead that night, became an instant fan. He would later compose "Naked in the Rain" (for the smash 1975 Crosby and Nash album, *Wind on the Water*) about Mr. McCord after watching him put on his make-up prior to a performance in the early Seventies at Mickey's ranch in Novato.

Joe and Jerry knew each other as far back as the mid-Sixties. The Warlocks and, later, the Grateful Dead, performed four benefits for the Mime Troupe between November, 1965 and April, 1967— to raise bail for the troupe and to fund their activism. McCord and Garcia were intimate friends from 1970 on. "We started hanging out again during *Tarot* {Joe's acclaimed Berkeley theater production that combined mime, music and satire}. I collaborated with Jerry, and he and I worked on my play, *Tarot*, which went from Berkeley to Broadway."

(Tom Constanten left the Grateful Dead in early 1970, in part, to write music for *Tarot* and to perform with the house band; Jerry would often show up unannounced before performances in Berkeley and sit in.)

"Jerry and I were very close. He was very selective about his friends. Jerry wasn't exactly the biggest social bee," admits Joe, uncorking a deep laugh. "He had a lot of 'pet peeves' and I was one of them. He was very visual, and I fit his visual world like a hand in a glove."

In the early 1970s, Joe was opening for the Dead at a Chet Helms-promoted gig when then-Grateful Dead manager Jon McIntyre and Jerry visited him backstage. They asked what the notoriously-cheap Helms was paying him and after Joe told them, Garcia reached into his pocket and handed him $500 in cash.

During the last 25 years of his life, Jerry and Joe held countless midnight-to-dawn "raps" (as the guitarist termed them) at Garcia's various homes. "Jerry left me with a legacy that I have to exorcise," says McCord. "We used to talk about the long, strange trip. About that picture of him above the 'For Rent' sign. We both believed, and would talk about, an artist being for rent, but not for sale."

They would also smoke a lot of pot. "Always joints," notes Joe, another robust laugh emanating from his belly. "Jerry got a kick out of the fact that I could roll a joint with one hand."

What kind of joint did Jerry roll ? "Perfect. Like a machine had made it. No bubbles or loose ends. He rolled them like a riff on his guitar."

Joe's middle name is Lennon, and spelled exactly the same as the late Beatle's last name. His parents were card-carrying Communists who wanted their son to have the middle name Lenin but instead compromised on the Lennon spelling for fear of government reprisal.

Mr. McCord's life is intertwined with the histories of performance theater, the Haight-Ashbury, the Grateful Dead, the Sixties, and the present: one of Joe's seven children, Orpheo McCord, is the percussionist in Edward Sharpe and the Magnetic Zeros.

It's interesting to note that, for a mime, Joe did not speak until age six. His parents had been taking him to see various specialists and sending him to different schools but nothing worked. His voice was finally activated after they took him to the local cinema to see *City Lights*, the classic 1931 film from, ironically, Charlie Chaplin.

After being asked why he had not spoken sooner, Joe told his mom, "I had nothing to say."

April, 1971

Many Deadheads and music fans alike assume it's Jerry playing the pedal steel guitar on "One Toke Over the Line," the 1971 Top Ten hit from Midwest duo Brewer & Shipley.

Is it really a misconception ?

Jerry did play pedal steel on the single's B side, "Oh, Mommy" (a call for President Richard Nixon to resign), laying down an ol' fashioned, rip-roaring country and western introduction. "Oh, Mommy" also features JGB stalwarts John Kahn on bass and Bill Vitt on drums.

Both "Oh. Mommy" and "One Toke Over the Line" appear on Brewer & Shipley's highly-regarded 1970 album, *Tarkio*.

"One Toke Over the Line" caused Vice President Spiro Agnew to lambaste the tune as "blatant drug-culture propaganda" and "subversive to America's youth." Further, he claimed, the song "threatens to sap our national strength," which led Nixon to place Brewer & Shipley on his "enemies list." (To this day, it's something they bring up — with pride — from the stage.)

In 1971, singing duo Gail Farrell and Dick Dale performed a gospel version of "One Toke Over the Line" on "The Lawrence Welk Show." After the two were done, Welk, unwittingly, but somewhat comically, referred to the song as a "modern spiritual."

So, if it's not Garcia playing pedal steel on "One Toke Over the Line," who is playing those sweet, countrified licks ? One possibility is the legendary Mike Bloomfield, as Paul Butterfield, a bandmate of Bloomfield's, appears on *Tarkio*. But Bloomfield is known as an electric blues guitarist and not for his pedal steel work.

The smart money is on John McFee, a long-time Bay Area session musician who played pedal steel and six-string guitar on albums by Mike Bloomfield, Boz Scaggs and the Grateful Dead ("Pride of Cucamonga" on 1974's *From the Mars Hotel*) before joining the Doobie Brothers in 1979. Another candidate is Pete Grant, a local session pedal steel player who was also a friend of Garcia's.

Since *Tarkio* was recorded at Wally Heider Studios in San Francisco, it's also possible that Buddy Cage, who replaced Jerry in the New Riders in 1971, cooked up those tasty licks.

Is it out of the question that Jerry is the unnamed, and uncredited, player ?

Not at all.

It sure sounds like him.

But so did the guitarist who played on the Edie Brickell and the New Bohemians' hit, "What I Am."

In 1969, Garcia began to teach himself to play the pedal steel guitar. "He dove into [it] like diving into a swimming pool without even checking the water," Pete Grant told *No Depression*.

SET ONE

Jerry's pedal steel work shows up on approximately 20 different albums, including LPs by artists as diverse as Link Wray, the Jefferson Airplane and Paul Pena. He plays pedal steel on two Grateful Dead albums (*Workingman's Dead* and *American Beauty*) and two Dead solo albums (*Garcia* and *Ace*). His pedal work is found on just three dozen or so different studio songs, the most famous being CSNY's "Teach Your Children" and the best being Graham Nash's "I Used to Be a King."

On the Nash masterstroke, from 1971's seminal *Songs for Beginners*, Jerry perfectly echoes the remorse Nash sings with as he tells his sad tale of regret. These were the songs Garcia connected with on a personal level: the down-and-out tales, the stories of despair and destitution. His austere, and subtle, playing on "I Used to Be a King" would steal the song were it not for the yearning, and hurt, in Graham's voice.

Garcia's pedal steel playing is found on about a half-dozen Grateful Dead songs (including "Dire Wolf," "High Time," "Candyman" and "Broke-down Palace") and the Dead solo tunes "Looks Like Rain" and "The Wheel." There are no studio recordings of Jerry playing the pedal steel after 1973. He stopped playing the instrument altogether in 1974, a hiatus that lasted until the Bob Dylan/ Grateful Dead tour in the summer of 1987, when Garcia broke out his pedal steel for Dylan's performances of "I'll Be Your Baby Tonight" and "Tomorrow Is a Long Time."

During Brewer & Shipley shows in 2007, the duo dedicated performances of "One Toke Over the Line" to Jerry, adding credence to the belief that it was Garcia on the song.

However, during tours in 2013 and '15, Mike Brewer made it clear from the stage that Jerry "played on this song's B side" before launching into "One Toke Over the Line," the pair's career-defining hit, which peaked at a lofty No. 10 on *Billboard*'s Hot 100 chart in April, 1971 — with or without Jerry on it !

November 14, 1971

Why is "Jack Straw" unequivocally one of the Grateful Dead's greatest and most-beloved songs ?

For starters, the vignette unfolds in a circular manner, with the Hunter lyrics "We can share the women/ We can share the wine" bookending the tale of two disparate souls on the run across the Midwest and Southwest, the sun so hot, the clouds so low ...

Its graceful opening notes and chords and the kind sensibility of its first line immediately endear "Jack Straw" to Deadheads. Hunter sets our imaginations afire with images of a Butch Cassidy and Sundance Kid-like duo fleeing through the Heartland. The lyricist also captures "the road is life" spirit of the Grateful Dead and the on-the-road adventure that compels Deadheads.

The song was one of the most exciting openers performed by the Dead, allowing the band, individually and collectively, to get loose early on. There was also Jerry's seditious solo during the bridge, which ignited our souls with its tenacity and fervor.

The longer the solo, the better !

The compelling morality plays within the novella force us to wrestle with our conscious and convictions: Play for money or life ? Settle one old score over one small point of pride or move on ? Cut your buddy down or suffer an undeserved fate because of that person's recklessness ?

"Jack Straw" also touches on themes popularly found in Hunter's thought-provoking lyrics: the struggle between good and evil; tales of episodic traveling; riding the rails, rolling the die and cutting the cards; the consequences of one's behaviors; life in America, and life on the road.

Although "Jack Straw" was considered by Weir for his 1972 solo debut, *Ace* (there's a rare outtake from the sessions of an acoustic version sung in its entirety by Bobby), Hunter had envisioned "Jack Straw" as part of a studio album titled *Ramblin' Rose*, which would have followed *Workingman's Dead* and *American Beauty*.

Instead, the song ended up on *Europe '72*, with the lines of Shannon and Jack Straw alternately sung by Jerry and Bob. When the Grateful Dead first began performing "Jack Straw" in 1971, Bobby sang both Shannon and Jack Straw's lines; a great example of a live version featuring Bob handling all the vocals can be heard on tapes of the Dead's gig at Texas Christian University on November 14, 1971.

Of "Jack Straw," a Deadhead blogger once astutely surmised: "There's no 'Detroit Lightning out of Santa Fe' and the Union Pacific — not the Great Northern — is 'out of Cheyenne' *but who cares ?* The Dead lay their musical filigree over, under and around Hunter's lyrics, merging the tale of Jack Straw with all the other legends of the American West."

1972

David Bowie had some interesting observations to make about Jerry after the guitarist's name came up in a 1972 interview with *New Musical Express*.

Bowie and a journalist are discussing the terms that rock journalists tend to overuse when the scribe mentions the word "camp" — as in sophisticated entertainment or effeminate mannerisms and definitely not as in what Boy Scouts and Girl Scouts do.

The interviewer observes that "punk," "camp" and "funk" are currently the three most trendy words among journalists, prompting Bowie to disparage the press for their "general inarticulacy" while also labeling them as "small-minded."

Bowie goes on to add, "I don't think I'm 'camper' than any other person who felt at home onstage, and felt more at home onstage than he did offstage."

That prompts the journalist to state, "Nobody ever called Jerry Garcia 'camp.'"

To which Bowie replies, "No, right, but he's a musician and I'm not a musician. I'm not into music, you see, on [his] level. I don't profess to have music as my big wheel."

Considerable praise from the Thin White Duke.

As an aside, in October 1972, director Mick Rock filmed an MTV-style music video for the Bowie song "The Jean Genie," blending concert and studio performances of Bowie and the Spiders from Mars with shots of the singer posing at the Mars Hotel in San Francisco with Cyrinda Foxe, a Warhol associate who would later marry Steven Tyler of Aerosmith. The Mars Hotel, the same building depicted on the cover of *From the Mars Hotel*, was selected because of its "street vibe."

November 5, 1972

Robert Hunter envisioned a studio album titled *Ramblin' Rose* as the follow-up to *Workingman's Dead* and *American Beauty*, which would have completed a trilogy of acoustic, harmony-graced LPs. Instead, the songs written for *Ramblin' Rose* almost all appear on two live Grateful Dead albums as a result of the constant pressure from Warner Brothers to provide the label with material to release.

Had the Dead fended off Warner, and instead gone into the studio in 1971 to record an album to follow *American Beauty*, songs such as "Wharf Rat" and "He's Gone" would have found their way onto a studio release. "To me, all [of] that material was the follow-up album to *American Beauty*," Hunter told Grateful Dead historian Blair Jackson in 1991.

The "material" Hunter is referring to — the tunes intended for the *Ramblin' Rose* album — were, regretfully, spread out over the subsequent live albums *Grateful Dead* (September, 1971) and *Europe '72* (November 5, 1972) as well as *From the Mars Hotel*.

According to Dead musicologist Osty Gale, the *Ramblin' Rose* album would have featured ten songs totaling nearly a full hour of music and this track list:

side one:

"Pride of Cucamonga"
"Bertha"
"Jack Straw"
"Mr. Charlie"
"Brown-Eyed Women"

side two:

"Tennessee Jed"
"Wharf Rat"
"The Stranger (Two Souls in Communion)"
"Ramble on Rose"
"He's Gone"

"I personally would've liked to hear those songs on an album of their own," Hunter told Mr. Jackson.

"Pride of Cucamonga" was written by Phil and lyricist Bobby Petersen and "The Stranger (Two Souls in Communion)" by Pigpen.

The thought of the Hunter trilogy is profound. Had the Grateful Dead gone into the studio and recorded those ten tracks as an album, the result would have been a broad masterstroke, especially when weighed within the context of a trilogy, and re-written the story of the Dead as a studio band.

Workingman's Dead and *American Beauty,* back-to-back masterpieces and the Grateful Dead's two most critically-lauded releases, confirmed Hunter's genius as a songwriter: He wrote or co-wrote 17 of the 18 songs on the two LPs. Hunter and Garcia also cemented their creative brilliance as a songwriting duo by co-writing 14 of the 18 tunes.

History would have held Hunter's trilogy in the same light as Bob Dylan's trifecta of *Bringing It All Back Home, Highway 61 Revisited* and *Blonde on Blonde.*

March 8, 1973

Ron McKernan was the heart and soul of the Grateful Dead during his seven-year reign in the band.

Pigpen set the on-stage demeanor for the Dead while bonding with Deadheads in a very real way. "He really had a connection with the audience that was unbelievable," recalls long-time Grateful Dead employee Steve Parish. "He would really grab them."

Mr. McKernan ruled the stage. Jerry and the rest of the gang were just walking in the shadow of his greatness. Pigpen allowed Garcia to do what the guitarist was most comfortable doing: play sideman. Pig was responsible for the edict the Grateful Dead and their individual members adhered to then and stick by to this day: We perform to serve the music and respect the audience.

His moxie emboldened the band, giving them confidence and swagger. When Bobby took on his "rock star" persona in the 1970s and '80s, there's no denying he copped his moves, and most of his bravado, from Pigpen. The one thing Weir couldn't steal — try as he may — was Pig's legendary ability to extemporaneously rap onstage.

Like Robert Johnson, Howlin' Wolf, Muddy Waters and every great Delta and Chicago bluesmen, the Grateful Dead's original keyboardist didn't just sing the blues, he lived them: the hardscrabble life, the damaged women, the battles with the demon alcohol …

His "soul mate" on this planet was, fittingly, Janis. No one else was man enough to step up to the plate and be her man, save for Pigpen. When they got down, according to Bobby, Pig would send her into the throes of ecstasy, with Janis screaming, "'*Daddy ! Daddy ! Daddy ! Daddy !*'

"When Janis came over [to our Forest Knolls summer camp], I didn't get a lot of sleep !"

"I've often wondered if that [John Barlow] line in 'Looks Like Rain' — 'street cats making love' — was inspired by [them]," asked Phil during a "Weir Here" podcast from TRI Studios in 2013.

From the very beginning, Pigpen was a natural-born leader onstage. His first band, an electric r'n'b and blues outfit named the Zodiacs, which came together in 1962, featured one of his future Grateful Dead bandmates serving as nothing more than a sideman.

"I was 16," recalled Pigpen. "We were playing beer-drinking fraternity parties at Stanford, doing Jimmy Reed tunes. Ron Ogborn would play the drums and I'd sing and play harmonica. Troy Widenheimer, who ran Dana Morgan Music in Palo Alto, played lead. His old lady Sherry played rhythm.

"Garcia would sit in on Fender bass."

May, 1974

Sue Stephens — like Eileen Law, Bob Bralove, Frankie Accardi-Peri and Ram Rod Shurtliff — is another of the many behind-the-scenes faces integral to the Grateful Dead's success story whose contributions are largely overlooked.

Ms. Stephens was hired as a Dead office assistant by then-Garcia manager Richard Loren in May, 1974, also serving as Jerry's bookkeeper. According to writer Matt Mattei, her duties included "paying Garcia's bills and handling his checking account."

Fun, and interesting, work, I imagine, *if* you can get it.

Eventually, Ms. Stephens went to work exclusively for Jerry, attending to the Garcia estate until 1999.

Jerry was so fond of Sue that he walked her down the aisle at her Marin wedding in 1990. In a photograph, he appears very happy to be serving such a role, smiling as he walks with Sue, hand-in-hand, dressed in jeans, a jacket and — don't you *ever* doubt it — a black T-shirt.

Sue described Jerry to Mr. Mattei as a "wonderful soul with a great sense of humor."

In one of the more apt, and interesting, descriptions *ever* of Garcia, Sue told Mattei: "They called him the 'reluctant Messiah.' He didn't want to be the leader. He just had that quality. He was such a creator and an intelligent, wonderful man."

She remembers the last time she saw Jerry: "[He] told me he was going to spend 21 days at Serenity Knolls. He said that he had picked that place out because it was an old Boy Scout camp that they used to crash at in the old days," Sue told *Rolling Stone* scribe Anthony DeCurtis. "When he left here that day, he stopped and gave me the biggest bear hug. He gave me one of those big bear hugs and told me to take good care of myself."

November 5, 1974

Jerry once turned down the opportunity to have John Lennon sit in with him during a Garcia-Merl Saunders show at New York's fabled Bottom Line nightclub on November 5, 1974.

Still deep inside his "Lost Weekend" period, Lennon had taken up with a reckless crew known as the

"Hollywood Vampires," who included Keith Moon, Harry Nilsson, Alice Cooper, Mickey Dolenz and Ringo Starr.

Lennon's Lost Weekend bender came to a head March 12, 1974, when John and Harry Nilsson were escorted out of Los Angeles' iconic Troubadour nightclub for relentlessly heckling the poor Smothers Brothers. "I got drunk and shouted," Lennon would later confess. "It was my first night on Brandy Alexanders — that's brandy and milk, folks. I was with Nilsson, who didn't get as much coverage as me, the bum. He encouraged me. I usually have someone there who says 'OK, Lennon. Shut up.'"

The Bottom Line, despite being open for just nine months, had already earned a reputation as the Village's hippest music venue. Co-owned by Stanley Snadowsky and Allan Pepper, Lennon was let in early by Pepper and, with 23-year-old Bronx-born budding singer-songwriter Melissa Manchester in tow, sat down at the center table Pepper had set up for him.

John then proceeded to snort cocaine all night (Manchester refrains) while chatting about the Grateful Dead with 22-year-old college student Stephen Bykowsky, who recalls Lennon mentioning *Wake of the Flood*.

By now "legless," as the Irish would say, John sends word to Jerry's "people" that he'd like to sit in. According to Blair Jackson's sensational biography, *Garcia: An American Life*, band bassist John Kahn recalled, "Lennon asked if there was a guitar there louder than Garcia's. Well, that got back to Jerry and Jerry said, 'No, fuck him.'"

"Jerry often talked with me about this evening," states Manasha Garcia (nee Matheson), Garcia's partner of six years. "He said that alcohol was the issue, John had been drinking heavily. When we spoke at length about the night, Jerry said that John was most likely distraught over his separation from Yoko.

"He told me that he'd wished he'd played with him. Jer loved and respected John as an artist. He held deep regrets and expressed them to me more than once."

A little more than three weeks later, on November 28, Lennon made his last public performance, during an Elton John concert at the Garden on Thanksgiving evening.

November 5, 1974 II

Here's the perspective — 40-plus years later — of Stephen Bykowsky, the 22-year-old who spent the night alongside John at the Garcia-Saunders show.

Was a cold, damp evening as I headed for the Bottom Line on November 5. This was going to be the first of six shows seeing Jerry and Merl, three nights, two shows each night. I told my friend, Allan Pepper, that I needed tickets for all six gigs. He asked why, and I said, "'Cause each show will be different !"

SET ONE

West 4th Street and Mercer Street were abuzz as I arrived for the early show and made my way in. I was solo for the first performance, and would be meeting my friends Cliff Russ and Art Goldsmith for the late show. My dear friend, Cliff, had just had his leg amputated and I was worried about him waiting in line.

The early show was a breeze. Jerry's beard was back, and he was wearing a black turtleneck. As the show ended, Allan Pepper came and got me, telling me not to leave. "Wait for the place to empty, and I'll seat you," he said.

With just the waitresses cleaning up, Allan told me to sit at the round table, dead center, the table I knew as the VIP table. Sitting alone, Allan suddenly walks up and introduces me to John Lennon and Melissa Manchester and seats them next to me. John is dressed in the same green Army jacket he wore onstage during his final headlining concert (the "One to One" festival, a benefit for the developmentally disabled, held at the Garden on August 30, 1972). The jacket has two breast pockets, and he is wearing a denim shirt beneath it.

Drinks ordered, the conversation picks up quickly, with John peppering me with questions on the Grateful Dead's mystique, also telling me how jealous he is that Jerry can play a small club. He brings up his fascination with the Dead allowing their fans to tape their concerts, and mentions he's blown away by how they play a different show each night by varying the song selection. I mentioned Jerry would touch on Motown, which surprised John. Sure enough, Garcia opened the show with "Second that Emotion" !

At some point, I grabbed Allan and told him that my friend Cliff was waiting outside. Melissa, John and Allan gasped; Mr. Pepper told me to go outside and get him. He escorted me outside, where Lennon's white limo was parked diagonal to the corner. We spotted Cliff in line, got him in, and he joined Melissa, John and I for conversation. A few years later, sadly, Cliff passed away from cancer.

The doors now opened, the crowd came in. Everybody noticed John, and most came up, "spotted" him a joint, wished him well and moved on. With the show about to start, both of John's breast pockets were bulging with joints. Art Goldsmith got in, joined us at our table, made his introductions, and enjoyed the show. Art is now a Professor of Economics at Washington and Lee University in Lexington, Virginia.

As the show started, I noticed John pull out a "leather pouch" and spoon. Filled with coke, John dipped all night, although Melissa never partook. I am positive John had no contact with Jerry before the show, as it was a few songs before Garcia even noticed John. The guitarist actually rolled his eyes at me when he realized who was sitting next to me. The show was hot, and John loved the whole scene.

After the show ended, Allan whisked Melissa, John and I backstage so John could meet Jerry. There was mild chaos backstage, with a few folks looking to "re-tune" their high. Jerry was very social in the intro to John and Melissa, John bid some thanks for covering Beatle tunes, with some other light banter. Jerry mentioned that if John wanted to sit in the next night, he was more than welcome.

John agreed, then didn't show.

Regardless, the next two nights were just as awesome.

— Stephen Bykowsky

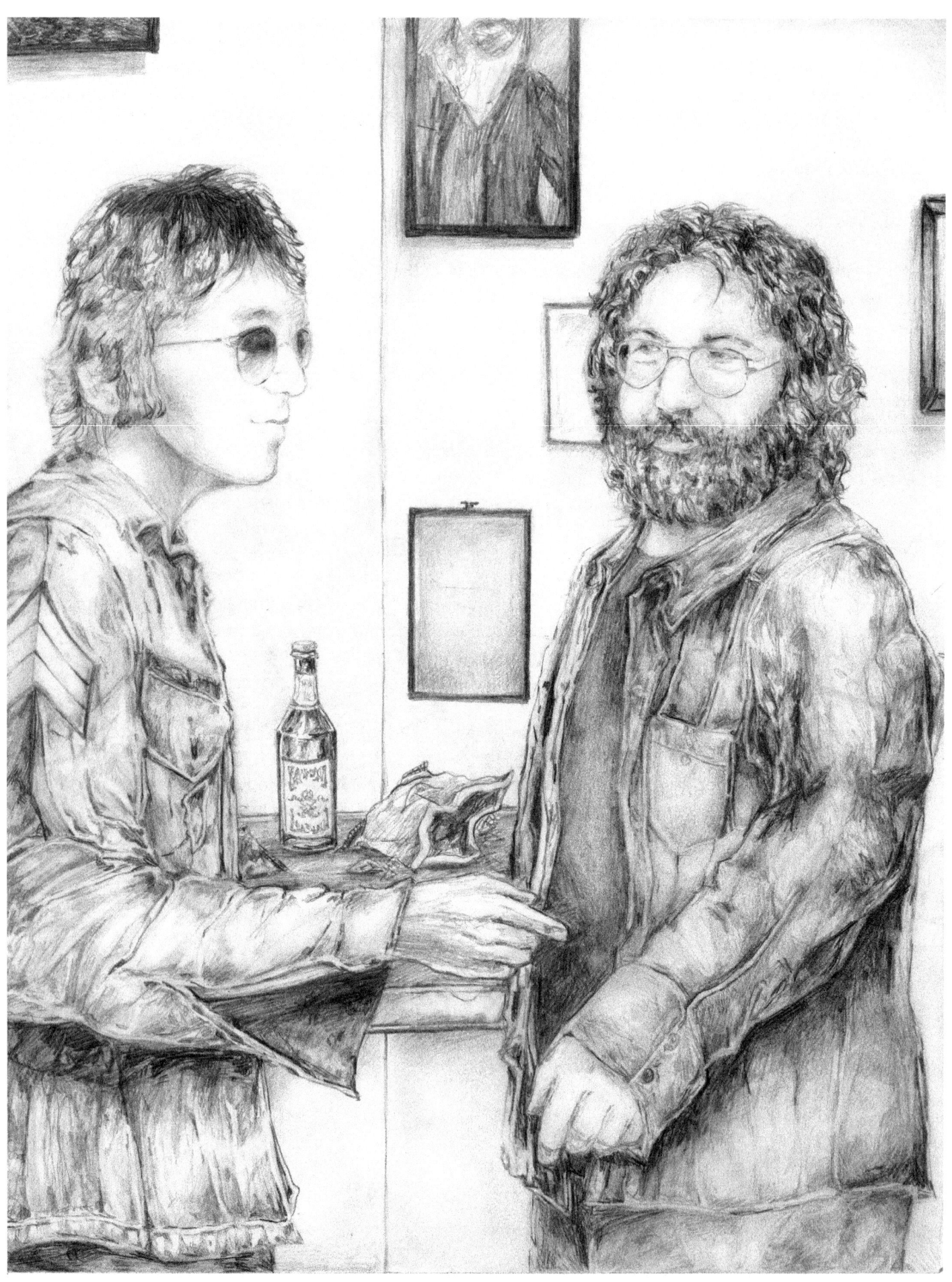

1975

Travis Bean was a California-based luthier and machinist whose guitars have been played by everyone from Jerry to Keith Richards, Ronnie Wood, Greg Lake, Slash and Stephen Malkmus of Pavement.

Garcia was first introduced to Travis Bean guitars in 1975, during the Grateful Dead's hiatus, and began to play several different models — first a TB 1000 and then a TB 500.

Jerry played the Travis Bean TB 500 onstage with the Grateful Dead in the summer of 1976, later using it to record *Terrapin Station*. He also played the TB 500 on the Grateful Dead's legendary 26-date spring East Coast tour in 1977, including the unparalleled three-night stretch of May 7 (Boston), 8 (Ithaca) and 9 (Buffalo).

According to totallyguitars.com, "Travis Bean guitars were known for their aluminum necks, which ran the length of the body. The guitar's pickups were fastened directly to the metal strip of aluminum, thus improving the guitar's sustain. The tone gave Garcia a nice bluesy overdrive which was missing from the more 'acoustic'-sounding Doug Irwin custom electric guitars he favored throughout [most] of his career."

One of Jerry's Bean guitars — a white version of the TB 500 — featured a red sticker (later replaced by a metallic one) at the base of the bridge that read: Ass, Grass or Gas Nobody Rides Free. That sticker had been placed over an earlier one that read: The Enemy is Listening.

Along with Irwin and Stephen Cripe, Mr. Bean, who passed away at age 63 in 2011, is one three renowned luthiers to have their hand-crafted guitars played by Jerry.

In 2013, Garcia's TB 500 was auctioned for $238,700, outselling Paul McCartney's 1964 custom Hofner bass at the same auction.

July 17, 1976

The Steely Dan song "Kid Charlemagne," written by Walter Becker and Donald Fagen for the band's 1976 album, *The Royal Scam*, was inspired by the life story of LSD pioneer Augustus Owsley Stanley III:

While the music played, you worked by candlelight
Those San Francisco nights
You were the best in town
Just by chance you crossed the diamond with the pearl

Owsley Stanley was a University of Virginia and Cal-Berkeley dropout and the paternal grandson of Augustus Owsley Stanley, a Kentucky politician who served the Bluegrass State as a congressman, governor and senator.

Owsley quit Berkeley to pursue the mass-production and distribution of high-quality LSD. According to *The New York Times*, "Mr. Stanley [was] an artisan of acid [who] turned out LSD said to be purer and finer than any other."

In the late 8th century, Charlemagne, also known as Charles the Great or Charles I, united most of Western Europe. He was king of the Franks and, later, the Lombards, before becoming Emperor of Rome in 800 AD. His reign was marked by his gift for leadership, which allowed people, and countries, to live in unison. Charlemagne's rule as Roman emperor lasted until his death at age 71 in January, 814. Today, he is recognized as the "Father of Europe."

Like Charles the Great, Owsley united a good part of the world. His LSD served as the electric circuit that ran through everyone and everything, connecting San Francisco, North America, Europe, most of the world and a universe or two with the heavens while instigating an intellectual, social and cultural quantum leap forward.

Owsley was also a benefactor to the Grateful Dead. In the summer of 1966, the five members of the Dead relocated to Los Angeles, where they lived in a three-story house on Third Avenue rented for them by Owsley. The experience of rooming together made them keenly aware of the positive effect it had on their practice habits and live performances.

The New York Times summed up Owsley's role with the Grateful Dead this way: "[He was their] soundman, early underwriter, principal acolyte, sometime housemate and frequent touring companion."

The Wall of Sound was created by Owsley and Dan Healy, and the Dancing Bear logo was designed by Owsley and graphic artist Bob Thomas, who drew the image. (Owsley once declared the bears should be known as the "Marching Bears" !)

Owsley, who died in a car accident at age 76 in March, 2011 while living in Australia, was honored by the Dead at their reunion shows in July, 2015 by having his ashes placed on their soundboard.

He was immortalized by Becker and Fagen in "Kid Charlemagne."

On July 17, 1976, Steely Dan's ode to Owsley, which features a scorching guitar solo from jazz legend Larry Carlton, peaked at No. 82 on the *Billboard* charts:

You turned it on the world
That's when you turned the world around
Did you feel like Jesus ?
Did you realize
That you were a champion in their eyes ?

May 8, 1977

On the afternoon of May 8, 1977, a bright 60-degree Sunday, the Grateful Dead were in town — Ithaca, New York, a college enclave on the southern tip of Cayuga Lake in the central part of the state — to perform at Cornell University.

"I wanted to see the town, so I arrived several days before the show," recalls Rick Bleier, a Deadhead who would celebrate his 27th birthday the night of the concert. "Ithaca is a beautiful place, a land of great natural beauty — amazing gorges, hills and waterways. One could sense the ghostly presence of [writer] Richard Fariña in the bars. The town pulsated with a wonderful bohemian energy."

The Cornell campus was abuzz as well, an excitement that had been brewing since last semester. Mike McEvoy, a Cornell Concert Commission member who later worked for Bill Graham, recalls, "I was responsible for booking the Dead. It took a lot of arm-twisting over many months, but [it] was well worth it."

A handful of lucky Cornell students, wearing red-and-white Concert Commission jerseys, were selected to serve as ancillary security for the Dead's show inside Barton Hall, the school's archaic athletic facility opened in 1915. Bustling across the campus commons, the "security force" dodged Frisbees being tossed at them by sun-loving students wearing shorts and sandals, many still hung over from last night's on-campus double-bill featuring Bronx-born comedian Robert Klein opening for vocalist Judy Collins.

The students weren't the only ones enjoying the sun. Inspired by the sparkling skies, the Grateful Dead spent part of the afternoon being driven around Ithaca in vans, rolling down the windows to hoot and holler with fans.

As the band cruised past the Moosewood Restaurant on North Cayuga Street, anxious Big Red underclassmen were inside enjoying the cafe's fine fare with their parents, in town to celebrate Mother's Day. The students were hopeful Mom and Dad would be gone by show time so their dresses and collared shirts and ties could be replaced by tie-dyes and jeans.

The doors to Barton Hall (capacity 5,000) opened late, forcing fans to wait outside for hours. The bright sunshine had given way to blustery conditions with temperatures plummeting into the low 40s. Sleet and rain began to fall. On a nearby grassy patch, a growing number of soaked fans gathered. LSD was being discreetly hawked, and bought, and business was brisk. An anonymous Cornell grad, quoted in a 2010 article about the concert on CornellChronicle.com, recalled: "I sold a lot of acid and bumper stickers [on what was] an eventful and unforgettable day."

When one of the two main gym doors was finally opened, frustrated fans shoved forward. Like clay being forced through a Play Doh toy, the lava-like flow of bodies was funneled into the door's tiny, rectangular opening. As the crowd surged, several concert-goers at the front of the line were lifted off their feet, as if caught in an undertow, while others were pressed into each other and the door's metal frames.

Despite the maddening crush to get in, not everyone was in such a hurry. "We broke into the building across from Barton Hall [because] of the weather, 100 or more of us, many tripping, and smoked pot in there until the doors cleared," reveals the same anonymous Cornell alum.

The crowd's push to get in made it impossible for the overwhelmed Concert Commission security force to properly frisk everyone and rip every ticket (unripped ducats still occasionally turn up on eBay, selling for hundreds of dollars). Security was instructed to confiscate cameras from fans, which is why photos of the concert are so scarce and another reason they couldn't properly search everyone. As a result, fans walked in with six packs, wine sacks, bongs and countless bottles of liquor.

The chaos also allowed the ticketless to sneak in.

SET ONE

Terrapin Station, released in July, 1977, was produced by Keith Olsen, noted for his work on *Fleetwood Mac* (1975). With the Dead, Olsen was a taskmaster in the studio, forcing them to rehearse endlessly, which had a major impact on their live performances during the spring of '77.

As the houselights fell inside the general admission event, the Barton Hall gym was already packed with Deadheads, students and locals, all partying hard, a good number tripping. The show began with the standard "Minglewood Blues" and right off, Garcia was tearing it up on his TB 500.

In an incendiary 12-song first set (clocking in at just under 90 minutes), the band hit their stride early with "Loser," "Jack Straw" and Weir's apropos cover of Merle Haggard's "Mama Tried" (after which Phil commented, "Thanks, Mom !").

Dr. Mark Nathanson, then an 18-year-old recent high school grad set to attend Oberlin College in the fall, drove nine hours from Sylvania, Ohio to attend the concert. He remembers: "During the intermission, I became really hot, and we were in the coolest spot in the gym. I had an Indian embroidered shirt made of fine white cotton that was drenched. We knew it was a really exceptional show, which definitely contributed to the perception of heat."

Nurturing the perception, and reality, that a great show was unfolding — a good number of Deadheads were tripping, creating a large-scale "contact high effect" inside tiny Barton Hall that fed the good vibes bouncing around the room.

By the time the Dead took the stage for the second set, as many as 6,000 people were crammed into the tiny gym, creating a sauna-like environment and forcing the band to perform their "Take a Step Back" routine to ease the jammed conditions in front of the stage. Even the normally reticent Garcia made a plea: "All these people in front are getting horribly smashed here. That means all you people in the back have to move back, or move back some."

As the cheery notes to the set two-opener, "Scarlet Begonias," kicked up, a late-arriving Cornell student who had been studying in the school library for a Monday morning accounting exam now less than ten hours away cut into the wedge in front of the stage created by those fans kind enough to "take a step back."

After pulling the tab back on a can of Genesee Cream Ale, the sophomore lit a joint. He spied his roommate and handed him a spare Genesee and the torpedo, rolled from a bag of primo $100 an ounce bud. Exhaling in a fit of coughing and smoke, he told his buddy, "You're not going to believe this, but it's snowing like crazy outside."

A new song, the reggae-tinged sermon "Fire on the Mountain," unknown to many in the crowd (the tune would fail to make the cut for *Terrapin Station*), segued seamlessly from "Scarlet Begonias," an in-concert pairing that would go on to work as well for the Dead as the coupling of Burns with Allen did for television.

In their epic one-hour-and-twenty-minute second set, the band played just six songs, skipping the drum solo, which fostered the set's runaway-train kinematics. According to Cornell alum Brad Krakow ('78), "You may notice this is one of the few shows that does not have a drum solo [and] I know why. Bill [asked me] if I had some drug I had never heard of, as his wrist was killing him ... I could barely afford beer back then, much less exotic painkillers. I mumbled something about looking for aspirin, and he went looking for a more supportive local."

The Dead nailed a 23-minute romp through "St. Stephen", "Not Fade Away", "St. Stephen" and, arguably, their best versions *ever* of both the "Scarlet", "Fire" couplet and Garcia's brilliant guitar elucidation, "Morning Dew."

"The second set's final 45 minutes or so ... *shazam* !" recalls Bleier. "I had seen the Grateful Dead a couple of dozen times prior to this, and I'd seen everybody else, and no one did what these guys did in concert. But this time it was clear they'd upped the ante. There was the sense that, somehow, things were being conceived, invented — the sorcerer's apprentices had riled-up them brooms — that perhaps anything could happen during the course of that time in that space. There was an enormous amount of inter-subjectivity going on at that show — the band looked amazed — and I have a clear-as-yesterday memory of Garcia's face as he shook his head and grinned from ear-to-Cheshire-cat-ear."

Was the May 8, 1977 show the greatest Grateful Dead gig ever ? Heck, some Deadheads believe it wasn't even the best of the three consecutive nights.

So, how did May 8 attain its legendary status ?

"First, and unquestionably, it was an extremely well-played show, an absolute instant classic," notes Charlie Rogers, a long-time Deadhead and Long Island native. "Cornell was the tape you'd hand to a newbie and say, 'This is what they sound like on a great night.' The concert was meticulously recorded by, among others, renowned Deadhead taper Jerry Moore, becoming the most-widely circulated tape among traders in the late '70s. Then, you add a cool concert poster {designed by graduating Cornell senior Jay Maybrey} and toss in a few salty tales about the travails of the weather, the problems getting in, and the *Animal House*-like debauchery going on inside. Finally, top it off with a killer set list and you have the legacy of May 8."

Dick Latvala, who served as the Grateful Dead's tape archivist from 1985 until his passing in August, 1999 (while also curating the *Dick's Picks* series of live archival releases), was constantly being asked by Deadheads when the May 8 show would be released. In a graveled voice, Latvala's standard response was, "Hell, everybody and his brother asks me that !"

Privately, Latvala had his own opinions. Of a May 22, 1977 show in Pembroke Pines, Florida (that closed with "Terrapin Station", "Morning Dew") two weeks to the day after May 8, he wrote in a journal kept to make show notations: "5-22-77 *tears apart* Ithaca. It rips it to shreds."

Most likely, "The All-Time Show" (if one could even exist) wasn't sold out, went down at an outpost on a weekday night, and was seen by a lucky few. Think: Missoula, Montana on a Tuesday (May 14, 1974).

As the last notes of the "One More Saturday Night" encore faded and the houselights came up, the crowd began to spill out through the same single door that only hours earlier had been the scene of a near-rampage. On each side were two huge, neatly piled four-foot stacks of garbage — mostly empty bottles, cans, plastic bags and food wrappers — still being crowned with refuse by the last of the exiting.

Outside, snowflakes, like tiny angels, gracefully fell from the night sky. Almost a half-foot of snow lie on the ground, nature affirming that something special had just taken place. (There were accumulations of 14 inches reported in some nearby areas.) Nathanson recalls, "I will never forget the sight of the shivering Deadheads in T-shirts, shorts and sandals huddled in the doorways of downtown Ithaca, trying to stay warm. It had to be 20 degrees that night."

"We were dazed children, glorying in the awe-inspired possibilities," says Bleier. "Just a block off-campus was Pop's Diner, where we made our way. It was filled to capacity with other hungry but contented Deadheads."

In May, 2014, Mr. Cary O'Dell, a curator with the Library of Congress, asked if I would be interested in writing an essay to accompany the enshrinement of the Grateful Dead's show on May 8 into the National Recording Registry.

An abbreviated, and edited, version of the-above essay appears on the Library of Congress webpage that honors recordings preserved in the National Recording Archive.

Here's the link:

https://www.loc.gov/programs/static/national-recording-preservation-board/documents/GratefulDead.pdf

Only 25 recordings are named to the National Recording Registry each year, based on a list generated by the Library of Congress.

Each of those recordings have been deemed by the Librarian of Congress, with input from the National Recording Preservation Board, to be so vital to the history of America — aesthetically, culturally or historically — that they demand permanent archiving in the nation's library.

May 11, 1977

Famed street artist and social and political activist Keith Haring sold his first piece of art in a place familiar to all of us — "Dead Mall" or, as it later came to be known, "Shakedown Street," the traveling caravan that followed the Grateful Dead from show to show, gathering in parking lots and local parks outside arenas before and after shows.

In the spring of 1977, Haring and his girlfriend decided to hitchhike around America to visit art schools. They hoped to fund their adventure, in part, by selling T-shirts that Haring and his roommate had designed featuring the Steal Your Face logo (which was, according to writer Jesse Jarnow, "altered with Haring's own instantly identifiable psychedelic squiggles") outside a Dead show on April 22, 1977 at the Spectrum in Philadelphia.

During the period 1976-78, Haring attended the Ivy School of Professional Art in Pittsburgh and worked at the Pittsburgh Center for the Arts, which allowed him to delve into the works of Jackson Pollock and Mark Tobey, among others.

While living in the Steel City, Haring had three life-altering experiences. He was turned on to LSD, fell in love with the Grateful Dead (spending one remarkable evening in his studio tripping, listening to the Dead, and drawing) and, in early 1977, attended a retrospective by the abstract expressionist Pierre Alechinsky.

Stoked by these experiences, Haring and his lady headed to Philadelphia for the show on April 22. There, the artist found modest success on Vendor's Row but achieved a first: his first publicly-sold work. Inside, the concert started off slowly but built in momentum throughout the evening, with the first set ending with a stellar "Playing in the Band." Set two kicked off with "Scarlet Begonias," "Fire on the Mountain," included the Dead's debut performance of "Got My Mojo Working" (the Preston "Red" Foster song made popular by Muddy Waters in 1957), and concluded with an epic "Terrapin Station."

Encouraged by his small but encouraging breakthrough on Shakedown Street and the incendiary show, Haring and his girlfriend set out to find America while the Dead embarked on the most-highly touted tour of their performing history.' "

On May 11, just three days after the Grateful Dead's heralded Barton Hall show on the campus of Cornell University, Haring accidentally crossed paths with the band and their caravan again; he happened to be visiting the Minneapolis College of Art and Design the same day the Dead were playing at the nearby Civic Center in St. Paul.

This time, the young artist, who had turned 19 one week earlier, and his unique T-shirt design found success in the parking lots. It was both an epiphany and an affirmation: he could make his way in the world as an artist.

Thrilled, Haring and his lady friend excitedly bought tickets and raced inside the Civic Center, where they were treated to a sizzling gig that featured first set takes on "Loser," "Jack Straw" and the always red-hot couplet "Lazy Lightning", "Supplication." Set two included another "Scarlet", "Fire" for the young couple as well as "Uncle John's Band" and a "Broke-down Palace" encore, an apt send-off for a brilliant young person on the precipice of greatness.

Haring relocated to New York City, where his subway drawings brought early notoriety. By 1980, he was holding exhibitions in Manhattan and by 1984 an international star.

At the height of the crack epidemic in the city, he created his most famous work, "Crack is Wack," a large mural on a handball wall located in a park on East 128th Street in East Harlem that is still visible from the south-bound lanes of the FDR Drive.

Keith would go on to set the art world on its ear with his radiant, colorful and provocative figure imagery. Mr. Haring died on February 16, 1990 at age 31 of AIDS-related complications.

In the spring of 2017, Haring's experiences in the Twin Cities and Grateful Dead world on May 11, 1977 became the subject of an exhibit at the Smallest Museum in St. Paul titled "Steal Your Face: Keith Haring and the Grateful Dead in St. Paul, 1977."

Perhaps, in the back of a drawer in an attic dresser, nestled next to your high school varsity jacket, lies an old Stealie T-shirt you purchased in the lot at a Philly or St. Paul show in the spring of '77.

If it's there, and not too tattered, you own a significant piece of art history created by a young Deadhead from Pittsburgh who dared to dream big.

July 4, 1977

In 1967, psychedelic "pop" bands emerged all over the world — London's Pink Floyd, the Doors in Los Angeles, Lou Reed and the Velvet Underground from New York, the Grateful Dead — grabbing the attention and capturing the imaginations of young people everywhere.

Pink Floyd and the Grateful Dead were, in many ways, mirror images, two pioneering psychedelic "pop bands" an ocean apart whose career successes and artistic growth and mythos paralleled each other's.

I was blessed to see Pink Floyd perform live twice — most memorably on the Fourth of July, 1977 at Madison Square Garden during their *Animals* tour. That night, on Seventh Avenue in front of the Garden, my brother Chris and I were fortunate to score two orchestra seats in the fourth row.

For a first set, the band played *Animals* start to finish. The pig props literally flew just feet above our heads. People were throwing and shooting off fireworks inside the Garden. It was both dangerous and thrilling ... the ultimate in live theater !

Set two consisted of *Wish You Were Here*, also played in album order.

The encore: "Money", "Us and Them."

I was ecstatic to hear some of the material from *Dark Side of the Moon* performed live; it was a seminal album in my youth, an LP that demonstrated the interconnectedness between the mind and music.

Seeing and hearing Floyd play those albums and songs, which I had spun over and over on my turntable, made the vinyl come to life.

We may have been just kids, but Chris and I were smart enough to realize we were witnessing one of the great rock bands at the height of their magnificent career.

Not long afterward, we saw the Grateful Dead perform for the first time. Having seen Pink Floyd, I was able to comprehend, and appreciate, the grand scope of the Dead in concert.

Chris and I took mescaline at Floyd in '77 and got off really well. Suffice to say, seeing Floyd on mescaline was a deeply fascinating experience but seeing the Grateful Dead on acid, well, that was a whole other level.

December 30, 1978

Of the many tales of debauchery that made backstage legends of the Grateful Dead, no tale is more outrageous than the story of the hedonistic soirée that went down before the Dead's infamous Pauley Pavilion gig on December 30, 1978.

As a result of the Dead's friendship with basketball Hall of Famer and renowned Deadhead Bill Walton, the band was finally allowed to use UCLA's spacious, and luxurious, team locker room (as opposed to the dumpy visiting team's digs) before their concert inside historic Pauley on December 30.

Even as one of the greatest Bruins ever, getting the UCLA athletic department to allow the Dead to use the locker room was no easy sell for Walton, as it had just been upgraded to a state-of-the-art facility, a costly, and municipally-funded, overhaul. But Walton's bubbly personality could win over folks as easily as J. Wellington Blimpy promising to "gladly pay you Tuesday for a hamburger today." To wit: Bill could convince legendary, and old school, UCLA basketball coach John Wooden to play Grateful Dead music while the Wizard of Westwood conducted team practices.

During the pre-show festivities inside the Bruins' locker room, a nitrous oxide tank emerged from beneath the cover of a tarp, with multiple hoses extending from the canister like snakes from Medusa's head.

The band and the backstage "glitterati" began to furiously work the tank, as if drinking elixir from a Fountain of Youth, huffing and huffing until, in no short time, the release valve froze.

The solution ?

According to Steve Parish's tome, *Home Before Daylight*, the crew hauled the canister, covered in white frost. into the Bruins' brand-new shower room, turned the valves to hot, and placed the frozen metal tank beneath the scalding water. Somewhat miraculously, this story doesn't involve a catastrophic, *Spinal Tap*-like moment involving the immolation of a drummer nor does it serve as fodder for the television show "1,000 Ways to Die."

But in a scene straight out of a Dirk Diggler movie, Parish recalls seeing several UCLA students follow the tank into the shower, where neither the red-hot water or the stares of a bemused Grateful Dead stopped them from feverously inhaling from the tank's serpentines. As the room slowly filled with the heat and humidity of a tropical rainforest, men and women alike begin to strip down to their undies and a wet T-shirt contest broke out. A handful of co-eds took it a step further, going commando. Chemistry, doing what it does best when steam and nitrous mix are mixed, depleted the oxygen supply, causing several people to pass out.

Because UCLA is a state school, it has a Board of Regents, whose members, along with a host of school and government officials, donors and athletic boosters, just happened to be on campus for a walking tour of the grounds. Timing being everything, the Board's stroll through the recently-upgraded men's basketball locker room coincided with the decision to heat the nitrous tank in the showers.

The troupe found themselves in a scene straight out of *Caligula*: An unconscious male Deadhead was laid out on his back, a full-on erection pointed at the ceiling like the Chrysler Building. Several half-naked male and female students were sucking on the tank's tentacles as if the hoses were offering free tuition. The Grateful Dead were sitting off to the side, passing around joints, amused by the sideshow.

The Dead were never allowed to use the home team's facilities in Pauley again.

May 9, 1979

My second Grateful Dead concert was also my first "on-the-road" Dead experience. On the morning of May 9, 1979, myself and two friends, with whom I had been drinking just eight hours earlier in a Bronx Irish pub, drove up to Binghamton, New York to see the band perform at the Broome County Arena.

The night before, my friends, Brendan Finn and Mary Callahan, and I had plotted our journey over tap beer and shots of Jack Daniels at the Hub on Fordham Road, owned and operated by a tough Irish-born former-amateur boxer named Gene Clarke. Even if Gene was a gentle giant, you didn't want to make any trouble in the Hub.

We assigned ourselves roles: Brendan would be Kesey, I'd take on Cassady's persona, and Mary was going to be Ann Murphy. We decided to pool our money to buy beer, weed and tickets, a plan hatched by the aptly-named Finn, a real huckleberry, a beer-guzzling, fun-loving junior at Fordham University, where I was a sophomore looking for the adventure, and trouble, Brendan could provide. He assured us that getting tickets for the show in Binghamton would not be a problem, even using the dreaded "guarantee" word. We drank until 2:00 a.m., till Mary and I began to act like two buzzed college kids, lasciviously eyeballing one another.

Mary's older sister either had sonar or a curious sense of timing, as her roommate suddenly materialized, fetching Mary and escorting the two of us from the Hub, me to my dorm, and, alas, Mary to her sister's apartment.

I felt like the hard-luck loser in a country song.

Mary, a sophomore at nearby Manhattan College in Riverdale, had huge brown eyes, long brown hair parted down the middle, a gleaming smile, and rarely wore a bra (it was the late Seventies). She was intelligent, wry and had a great sense of humor. I fell asleep looking forward to a great time with her and Finn.

On the ride up Route 17, Finn regaled us from the backseat of his father's Grenada with stories of having seen the Dead at upstate locales such as Syracuse and Utica. We were a rapt audience, having each seen the Dead exactly once. When Brendan wasn't telling tall tales, Mary and I were reading the *Times Herald-Record*, which we picked up at a gas station in Middletown. As I pored over the baseball boxscores, she commented on a story about the recent, and devastating, shutdown of the Remington Rand typewriter factory in Elmira, a small town just west of Binghamton, where 690 locals had gotten the ax. "Industry is abandoning the people up here," she said, adding, with bitterness, "Remington is moving its operations to Toronto and blaming the company's inability to recover from a four-month employee strike three years ago as the reason. How lame is that ?"

"That's the way it's been in town ever since they tore the jukebox down," said Brendan.

In the years to come, venturing north of the city to see the Grateful Dead in every small New York town, I fell in love with the entire upstate region, but my heart would break every time I saw another closed factory or an out-of-business sign in the front window of a store or shop.

Upon our arrival in Binghamton, the area around the coliseum was an absolute madhouse. It was a gorgeous spring day, with temperatures soaring into the high 70s, the Catskills were inquisitively looking down at the tie-dyed mass, and people were everywhere. The parking lots were packed, and we're informed it's a sell-out. We were lucky to land a parking spot. How are we going to find three tickets ?

I could tell Finn — normally, Mr. Confidence — was rattled, that this was definitely outside his normal Grateful Dead experience.

For me, this would be old hat if I were in Manhattan. I was used to tracking down tickets outside the Garden in the most-dire of circumstances — opening night for the Stones in June, 1975, Floyd on the Fourth of July, 1977, and Zeppelin's six-night stand in '77. There was always a scalper or fan on Seventh Avenue with a ticket for sale at reasonable market value.

Problem was, I soon figured out, there was no Bob from Binghamton or Albie from Albany scalping tickets. In fact, no one was scalping or sell tickets. And people had that look of desperation on their faces I had seen countless times outside sold-out Garden shows, a look that said: I am not getting in tonight.

Leaning against the Granada, Finn casually slugged a Miller; he didn't seem too concerned, jovially laughing like Nero while telling Mary and myself not to worry, that we were all going to get in. No longer in the cozy confines of my concrete jungle, I began to sense that Binghamton, even on a Wednesday night, was a town where everyone who bought a ticket to a big-time show like the Grateful Dead was going to use that ticket. I also realized, for the first time, that Deadheads don't give up their ducats, such is their love for the band.

We pooled what was left of our money: I had $40, Finn came up with a Jackson, and Mary, well, she had those big brown eyes. We decided to split up and search for tickets; Finn and I took $30 each and Mary went off on her own. We agreed to meet at the car in a half-hour. It was nearing 6:00 p.m. and the freneticism outside the arena was alarming. I stood by the entrance, hoping to find a 'Head who had a friend who dropped out at the last second. Sure enough, a guy with an extra walks over; his buddy decided he wanted to stay home to watch the NHL playoffs. He demanded $30. I knew I'd be left broke but I also knew at moments like this it's better safe than sorry. I bought the ticket.

As I turned away, a Deadhead was being ejected. A surly, muscled usher with "Ted" on his nametag shouted at him, "And don't try coming in here with that fake ticket again or I'll kick your ass and have you arrested." The usher threw the bogus ticket into a garbage pail and walked back in. I immediately retrieved it. A fake ticket was better than no ticket, I told myself. I was used to bribing my way into the Garden and figured if Finn got a ticket for $20, maybe we could hand an usher the fake and a $10 bill.

Back at the car, Mary could not hide her blues. Finn showed up with a ticket, but had also spent $30 on it. We immediately offered Mary our tickets but she would have none of it. "Give me the fake," she told us.

SET ONE

Finn and I may have only been barely 20 or so, but we knew better than to script any plan that didn't involve all three of us getting in. We talked about using an entrance where Ted wasn't working, hoping a different usher wouldn't notice the phony. But Mary kept insisting that she be allowed to try to get in using the fake. In a worst-case scenario, I figured, if Mary didn't get in, I'd talk Finn into going inside and sell the ticket I bought, use the money to buy more beer, and she and I would hang out at the car, drink beer, smoke weed, fall in love and forever remember May 9, 1979 as a magical night in our magical lives.

About to get in line, there were two distinct feelings in the air: joy among the ticket holders and despair among the ticketless. As we approached the entrance, to my utter dismay, I saw Ted move over to our slow-moving line to expedite the ticket-tearing process. I handed my ticket to him. He looked it over long and hard before tearing it in half and handing me the stub. I walked into the lobby and watched as Mary gave Ted the fake. "I'm sorry, young lady," I heard him say, "but this ticket is counterfeit."

My heart sank. I looked at Mary. Tears welled up in her big brown eyes. Her eyelashes batted a time or two and a single tear ran down her right cheek. Another streamed from her left eye. She looked up at the bulky man, clutching the fake in her hands, and pleaded in the softest voice, "Please, sir, I drove here from Elmira, where my dad just got laid off at the Remington factory. I spent all my money on this ticket. I have none left. If you could just …"

Mary didn't have to finish her sentence. The same man who was threatening to kick the Deadhead's ass and have him jailed just twenty minutes ago was now a big ol' sappy lug: "Well, that's alright, young lady. You stop your crying now, you hear? Elmira's a good town with good people and your daddy will find work. Big Ted is gonna look the other way and you just walk on in and enjoy your rock-n-roll concert."

Finn was next. Ted eyeballed him like a TSA agent sizing up the profiled at an airport baggage check. "Ticket," he gruffly demanded. Finn handed it to him. Ted, moved by his kind act, was a bit teary-teared. He didn't even look at the ticket, he just ripped it in half, shoved the stub at Finn, and gruffly remarked, "Cut your hair, son." Inside the lobby, the three of us excitedly hugged, a joy I can remember to this day.

"Never trust a Prankster!" exclaimed Brendan.

We ran to our seats on the side of the stage, settling in as the Dead opened with a 17-minute "Sugaree" followed by a "Take a Step Back" appeal from Bob. It was incredibly hot inside the jammed building; a lot of men were taking off their T-shirts; people would later claim the room temperature exceeded 100 degrees. We could see the action onstage up close and there were a half-dozen Hells Angels hanging out on the side, drinking Tall Boys and smoking joints.

Finn reached down into his pants and pulled out three Millers. "I told you we'd get in," he said, trying to sound convincing as he handed us bottles warmer than the arena.

Given our dire circumstances just 20 minutes ago, that beer tasted better than a chilled bottle of Dom Perignon.

The heat added to the raw, feral energy emanating from the stage. I recall an incendiary "China Cat Sunflower", "I Know You, Rider" to open set two, a furious, rampaging version with notes flowing from Garcia's guitar like boxcars railing across the Kansas plains at night. It became even more apparent to me that Jerry controlled and directed the music, armed with the gifts needed to captivate the Muse.

My other memory is of the drum solo: primitive and intense. Like Garcia and his magical guitar, Hart and Kreutzmann, I discerned, could use percussion to charm the Mysterious Creature. I sat enrapt and watched as Ramrod lit a fire inside a garbage can and warmed up and stretched out a tar (an African drum that originated in ancient Turkey), which he handed to Mickey, who made that tar *talk*.

On the ride back down Route 17, Mary and I sat in the backseat, like Neal and Ann Murphy, holding hands and sharing joints as a less-loquacious but wiser Finn drove, having learned: There are no "guarantees" in Grateful Dead world.

Although Mary and I never had our moment, didn't become life-long friends, or even have a first kiss, we were both beaming.

That night in Binghamton was the first time the magic of the Grateful Dead was put on full display for me, rearing up its mighty head and blessing my youthful soul.

March 30, 1980

Beloved comedian John Belushi joined the Grateful Dead onstage for their "U.S. Blues" encore at the Capitol Theatre in Passaic, New Jersey on March 30, 1980. It was Palm Sunday and, despite the holiness of the day, Deadheads were gathered outside the sold-out Capitol clutching wads of cash like rosary beads, frenetically looking for tickets.

Like characters in a Springsteen song searching for something in the night, you could feel their desperation. My friends and I sat down at a hole-in-the-wall across from the aged theatre and ordered beers and shots of Jack Daniels. Earlier, we had each taken a drop of liquid LSD. Behind the bar, a ticket for tonight's show was pinned between two smoky mirrors with a note beneath it that simply read: "$100."

We sat and drank and watched as the urgency outside increased with every passing moment.

Finding tickets in the parking lot at a venue was rarely an issue at a Grateful Dead concert in 1980, even at a sold-out, small theater show. Extra tickets were not only typically available, but they could easily be bartered for, which was the then-preferred method of payment between parking-lot Deadheads. Among the items of choice for trade: kind bud, custom-made turquoise and jade jewelry, tie dyes, posters, a back rub, and the always-popular "place to crash on my couch for a ticket" option.

Tonight, a place on a couch in a Waldorf suite wasn't getting you a ticket.

Eventually, an unlikely buyer — a hippie kid with a scruffy beard and a mane of curly locks — walked into the dive, slapped down a Ben Franklin, demanded the ticket from the barkeep, and ordered two shots of tequila. He handed the ticket and a shot to a friend and together they drank to their good, but costly, fortune. I heard the friend say, "Thanks, man, but you're outta your mind to drop that kinda bread on a ticket for me."

I was impressed by the young man when he replied, "You're welcome, man, but it's only money."

The Capitol show was the first time I sat up-close at a Dead concert. My 19th row seat allowed me to watch the band's on-stage interactions and tomfoolery. It was fascinating to watch Jerry smoke in between songs, or follow his hands during his solos, especially during "Althea."

John Belushi's appearance almost didn't take place. The Dead were more-or-less a democracy when it came to deciding who would be allowed to sit in with them; meaning, things could be voted on if Jerry was in favor. Phil was adamantly against the Belushi idea.

But Jerry, who got on well with Belushi, was in favor, so the band got to vote.

Phil was outvoted.

Belushi cartwheeled his way onto the stage for the encore; he was anything but inconspicuous, joining in on the background vocals for "U.S. Blues." His cartwheel immortalized the comic genius in Grateful Dead lore.

That evening, I was a 20-year-old voyager tripping on the good ship Life, an experience that would last well into the next morning, which I spent waiting in line at the Bursar's Office to pay my tuition.

Like the train ride home from the Garden, I was certain everyone around me knew I was high.

On April 5, the Dead got to hang out with Belushi again when they appeared on "Saturday Night Live" to promote *Go to Heaven*, performing "Alabama Getaway" and "Saint of Circumstance." The show was co-hosted by the husband-and-wife duo of Richard Benjamin and Paula Prentiss and contained a hilarious satirical sketch on Deadheads: neighbors with little in common suddenly bond after discovering they're all crazy about Joey Bishop.

May 8, 1980

The excited chirps of Deadheads, like the birds fluttering about them, filled the prescient air on May 8, 1980, a sparkling spring afternoon in upstate New York. The cherry and apple blossoms had finally begun to bloom in Glens Falls, a frozen-in-time town just north of Albany. The Grateful Dead were performing tonight at the local Civic Center, renowned as the annual host of the state high school basketball championships, the arena every New York hoopster dreams of playing in.

The ground outside the Civic Center was still hard from winter; the arrival of the Dead, a yearly rite in northern and western New York, signaled the coming of warm weather. Still, there was a nip to the air, which meant Deadheads selling their wares were bundled up despite a sparkling sun framed by blue skies. 'Heads were hawking beers from all over the world (always one of my favorite aspects of the lot scene), amazing hand-made tapestries, jewelry and beads, gems and stones, imaginative cassette tape covers and, of course, "good weed."

A few had extra tickets. "Who needs one ?" was a common refrain that afternoon. There were no "miracle ticket" seekers holding their fingers in the air, no factory-made tie-dyes, and no mention of any "drug" other than marijuana, LSD and mushrooms. Like the mountain air, the environment was crisp, free from pollutants, and invigorating.

The Civic Center has a unique feature: large plate glass windows that circle the top of its interior. As the show began, the curtains, which were normally drawn to block the light and maximize a band's stage theatrics, were left open. The Grateful Dead were never one to prioritize their "stage show" over the wonders of nature. Whenever possible, they synchronized their playing with the energies, experiences and sites around them; this night, the energy source was the calliope of colors oozing through the Civic Center's windows. As "the sun went down in honey" (to quote Barlow), the band fell into a graceful "Friend of the Devil."

At Fordham, I became good friends with Charlie Daly, a surprisingly laid-back guy for a hard-nosed Irish kid from Staten Island. The core of our close friends and classmates, including Finn, had graduated the previous spring, so Charlie and I were pretty much left to our own devices to keep ourselves entertained. Most days, when we weren't in class, we engaged in intense, and lengthy, games of backgammon. First, we'd pick up a nickel bag and a dollar's worth of Swedish Fish from Choc Zilia, a local Jamaican-run weed store on Marion Avenue that fronted as a candy store. The Jamaicans loved me because I was a regular, but I could tell it would drive them crazy every time I ordered ten red fish along with some bud. Over countless board battles, Charlie and I spun a limited rotation of albums: Neil Young's *Zuma*, *Workingman's Dead*, Warren Zevon's *Excitable Boy*, the Outlaws' *Hurry Sundown* and *The Marshall Tucker Band*. Occasionally, my roommate, Tom Whalen, a hip, bronzed Adonis who worked summers as a lifeguard on Long Beach, would slip in *Pet Sounds*. Charlie and I solidified our friendship with banter, humor, competition and one Choc Zilia joint after another.

We had driven north on a lark. At 21, I was blessed to be intelligent enough to prioritize the Grateful Dead, and its surrounding circus, as an integral life experience. Glens Falls is a straight shot up Interstate 87, about three hours from the Bronx. On the drive, I recall seeing, for the first time, the red, white and blue Steal Your Face logo painted on a granite boulder. In years to come, I came to think of that image and the large rock as the gateway to upstate New York; depending on which part of the state you were seeing the Dead in, you'd either stay on 87 or jump onto the Taconic Parkway or Route 17.

The band broke into "High Time," a song from *Workingman's Dead* that Charlie and I had listened to numerous times while playing backgammon; suddenly, a jolt of electricity surged from the stage, a small burst of energy that forcefully washed over, and through, us. Like a rugged wave crashing toward the shore, it literally knocked Charlie off his feet and into his seat. I could not fathom what I had just experienced. I looked at Chuck, and he was slumped over.

What was that ?

And did anyone else feel it ?

Months later, after transferring to the University of Oregon, I was at a Baba Olatunji concert at the W.O.W. Hall, once a meeting place for the Woodsmen of the World fraternal organization and now a small performance theatre. Late on a Saturday night, as Olatunji began to make the talking drum talk, what was left of the crowd (including Kesey, Babbs and a few of their crew), sat in a large circle in front of the stage, holding hands. This was exactly why I had come to Eugene — to experience the metaphysical and, for me, the unknown. I joined the group. Everyone began to *ohm*, a low hum that slowly rose in volume and timbre as Olatunji played along to our collective voice. *Voom !* The same flash of electricity that I had experienced months earlier in Glens Falls passed through me again, through everyone, I could tell. Only this time, no one got knocked on their ass and most everyone acted as if it was old hat.

After the Dead show, Charlie and I walked back to our rented car only to discover it had a flat tire and the cheap-rate rental joint on Webster Avenue had failed to supply a spare. This was the last thing Chuck needed, as he was still beat up from stepping on the third rail. We were parked in a Sinclair gas station; like most of the town around us, the decor was Norman Rockwell — the Art Deco diner across the street with a Coke machine out front, the manicured baseball diamond down the block, the red-brick facing of an office building, the Rexall drug store, and the porcelain Sinclair sign with its image of the friendly green Dino the Dinosaur, the street light reflecting off its patina as it flapped all night in the wind.

In many a small town the day after a Dead show, if you didn't clear out early, you could feel as conspicuous, and welcome, as a person without a hood at a KKK rally. The fella at the gas station looked us up and down, sniffed to see if we stunk any, and snickered when he asked, "Why didn't you college boys just use the spare ?" Indignation aside, it was all of two dollars to get the tire patched. We jumped onto 87 south and flew. That is, until a state trooper pulled us over. Still buzzing with that day-after-a-show high, it was all I could do not to stare at the trooper's purple tie, which was radiating like an arrow of neon out on the avenue.

Adding to Charlie's woes: a speeding ticket.

We still see each other, mostly at Fordham basketball games or Phil or Bobby shows. We've only talked about the Glens Falls "incident" once. Charlie laughed about getting bowled over, and I recalled how drained he was afterward. We never talked about it again, the same way two friends who shared the cost of a winning lottery ticket that one misplaced no longer discuss it.

I was all of 21 when I got zapped by the 13-point lightning bolt that night. Fortunately, youth was not wasted on me. I lived a zealous life when I was young and a good part of that living was done, thankfully, in the company of Deadheads and the Grateful Dead.

After I had enough time to put everything about the night of May 8, 1980 into perspective, I concluded: "There's something very peculiar about the Grateful Dead, and I am going to figure out exactly what it is."

May 16, 1980

I had been seeing the Grateful Dead for almost 18 months when I set up shop by myself in a cozy side-stage seat at the Nassau Coliseum on the evening of May 16, 1980 — my twelfth Dead show.

It was an interesting time for me, a period of transition. I had decided to leave the good Jesuit brothers at Fordham behind and head out west to attend the University of Oregon. I'd been weighing the pros and cons of the move for the better part of a year and it came down to the three "E's" — economics, education and environment. The tuition at Oregon, a state school, was a quarter of what I was paying to attend private Fordham, and my heart was set on a journalism degree, not one in mass communications. I had grown up in the Bronx and it was time for me to explore a town where, I was told, Kesey, Babbs and Mountain Girl freely frolicked.

As I sat in the Coliseum, rolling a joint and waiting for the lights to fall, I couldn't help but to rethink my decisions and the life path I was on. If I had learned one thing about a Grateful Dead concert to this point, it was this: It was a good place to think things through, if that's what you needed to do. At 21, part of me was convinced I was following Plan Nine from Outer Space. Transferring to Oregon was a hard sell to my parents, and I don't think they believed I was headed to Eugene until the morning I set out.

In the fall of 1979, I had seen my first succession of Grateful Dead shows — three consecutive nights at Nassau on Halloween and November 1 and 2. Brendan Finn and I went together on the 2nd and he was his usual jocular self, insisting we set a goal of sneaking down to the first row by the encore. I'm the type of concert-goer who prefers to sit in my assigned seat, as I learned as a kid that people tend to be very snooty, and even nasty, when they show up with tickets for the close-up seats you were certain you'd be occupying all evening.

Following Finn down the rabbit hole always guaranteed adventure, mischief and a ton of laughs. It was a Friday night and I knew he'd be in rare form, so I was all aboard. Brendan had a Neal Cassady quality to him: He could slam the cue ball into racked pool balls while holding a beer (which he never spilled), carry on multiple, and engaging, simultaneous conversations, and forge his own reality as he steamed straight ahead. By the time the Dead broke into "Casey Jones" as their encore (the only time I was lucky enough to hear them play the *Workingman's Dead* beauty), as Finn promised, our asses were squarely planted in "the front row," as the great Bob Uecker would say !

When I first became a Deadhead, I was aware the Grateful Dead played a song titled "Morning Dew," vaguely recalling it as part of the long, drawn-out sixth side of *Europe '72*. But I had never heard them play it in the eleven shows I had seen to this point.

I had witnessed numerous rock groups scale mountaintops live, with virtuosic guitar performances of their most epic works: Steve Howe of Yes laying it on the line during "Starship Trooper," Keith Richards torching "Midnight Rambler," Allen Collins of Lynyrd Skynyrd soaring on "Freebird," and Zeppelin's Jimmy Page tearing it up on *Physical Graffiti* tunes such as "Ten Years Gone" and "In My Time of Dying."

Despite those experiences, nothing could've prepared me for the first time the Grateful Dead, and Garcia in particular, pulverized my mind with their reading of "Morning Dew" on May 16, 1980.

As Jerry drew the opening notes and chords to the Bonnie Dobson composition, I was buried in thought, having spent the night, to this point, reviewing every aspect of my goals for the next few months. It was cathartic to hear Jerry play "Morning Dew." By the time he wrapped it up with his declaration of "I guess it doesn't matter, anyway," I no longer thought about my plans with uncertainty or apprehension. I had emerged cocksure and emboldened, a long-haired, shaggy-bearded Davy Crockett in tie dye.

In my short time as a Deadhead, I had witnessed Garcia's wizardry and realized that he was connected to a higher source; how, or for what purpose, I wasn't entirely sure.

The late, and brilliant, guitarist Allan Holdsworth — using words that apply to Jerry — once said of John Coltrane: "It was almost like he had found a way to get to the truth, somehow, to bypass all of the things that ... you have to face."

June 19, 20 and 21, 1980

"Seems like I've been here before," sings Weir in "Born Cross-Eyed."

That lyric proved to be true when Bobby returned to Anchorage, Alaska nearly four decades after the Grateful Dead performed there in 1980 to sit in for an ailing David Nelson for three shows by the David Nelson Band on March 16-18, 2017 at the Sitzmark Bar & Grill in Girdwood, a resort town in Anchorage.

Bobby, the epitome of class, once again demonstrated why Jerry privately referred to him as a "prince."

Typical of their Zeitgeist, the curious timing of a celestial event at their 1980 shows demonstrated what a long, strange trip it really could be for the Grateful Dead.

Inside the tiny auditorium of Anchorage's West High School (seating capacity: just 2,000), the Dead played a series of shows — their only Alaska gigs — on June 19, 20 and 21 that coincided with the Summer Solstice.

At the exact moment of the solstice — 9:37 p.m. AKDT on June 20 — the band was onstage, deep into a second-set segue of "Estimated Prophet", "The Other One."

Northern Stage Co., which promoted the shows, was run by Skip Lichter and his brothers, George and Andy, who rolled out the red carpet for the Grateful Dead. "We had the band up for a couple [of] weeks," Skip told writer Chris Bieri of the *Anchorage Dispatch News*. "We had a lot of activities planned. We brought everyone up to the top of Rabbit Creek at Hash Hill and had a special dinner of salmon, halibut and caribou stew."

The *Anchorage Times* detailed the activities: "Mickey Hart immediately flew out to go salmon fishing, while Weir and Brent Mydland took a flight-seeing tour that included Mount Susitna and Knik Glacier."

The *Times* ran a photo of Billy chewing on a large block of Columbia Glacier ice while the *Dispatch News* reported Bobby and Phil took a flight in a news radio helicopter to do a spoof traffic report: "On Tudor Road headed eastbound, in the area of Muldoon, everything seems to be moving right along, but traffic appears to be going backwards," Bobby was quoted as reporting. "[Drivers should] turn on your lights and honk your horn."

Lichter recalls seeing two 18-wheelers truck the Dead's gear up the Alcan Highway. Lewis Leonard, another local who also attended the 1980 shows, says of the gigs: "Literally, the room was kind of a speaker in itself. It was incredible sound." Lewis tripped on the night of the Solstice: "[The sound] was *so* good that I dropped acid [on the] second night."

Sitting in for Mr. Nelson at the Sitzmark almost four decades later, Bobby looked and sounded great, playing both acoustic and electric guitar for the shows while performing a mixture of material. Included were Weir solo tunes ("Gonesville," "Blue Mountain," "Mexicali Blues"), Grateful Dead songs ("Stella Blue," "Ramble on Rose," "Shakedown Street") and Dead covers ("Walkin' Blues," "Iko Iko," "Big River").

Mr. Weir's hair and beard were smartly groomed and he was sporting a snazzy pair of eyeglasses. On the 17th, he wore a black T-shirt in the style of his late friend, a cat named Garcia.

David Nelson, who is battling colon cancer, has a superb backing band featuring an aged cast of tried-and-true Bay Area talents: bassist Pete Sears (who auditioned for the Dead in 1990 as a replacement for Brent), drummer John Molo, keyboardist Mookie Siegel and six-string and pedal steel maestro Barry Sless, one of the top jamband guitarists in the game today. They were joined all three nights by vocalist Katie Skine, who lent a delightful touch to the music. The group was both cohesive and electrifying, with locals reporting Bobby and the Nelson Band took to the stage each afternoon while the bar was open to rehearse in front of the Sitzmark patrons, bringing new meaning to "Happy Hour."

Over the course of three shows, the quintet delivered a slew of dazzling moments, including "China Cat Sunflower", "I Know You, Rider" to close the first set on the 16th, a gorgeous "Stella Blue," replete with mournful pedal steel work from Mr. Sless, on the 17th, and a "Friend of the Devil " true-blue to the *American Beauty* version on closing night.

Ironically, it was Skip Lichter, today a talent buyer and music consultant for Alyeska Resort (which promoted the Nelson Band shows), who first heard from Bob. "This isn't a big money-making thing and neither were the shows in 1980," says Lichter. "Those were to get [the Grateful Dead] to experience Alaska."

West High is built on a bluff that overlooks the sprawling Chugach Mountains. The view of a distant valley is breath-taking. Below, the dark waters of a murky lagoon lend an ethereal touch. Not long after the Dead played the school's auditorium in 1980, stories began to circulate around Anchorage of a ghostly apparition appearing inside the school.

In 2015, an article on americanghoststories.com claimed the auditorium has since been haunted by a "Lady in White." The author wrote, "She is sometimes seen standing in silence among the seats of the empty auditorium, as if she is waiting for the show to begin, sometimes just escaping through corridors as if she is running from something, sometimes lurking around the corners backstage or in the dimly lit basement halls."

Like the Lady in White, good-guy Weir's circuitous Alaskan experiences, spanning almost 37 years, can best be summed up by another lyric from "Born Cross-Eyed" — "Think I'll come back here again/ Every now and then from time to time."

October 3, 1980

On the morning of October 4, 1980, I woke up in a cow pasture in Northern California, just outside Eureka, with no money, no wallet, and no recollection of what had gone on the night before. I wasn't wearing my jacket and both my cap and backpack were missing. Worse, I had no idea how I got there.

SET ONE

My first conscious thought: I had been the victim of a UFO abduction. To my relief, when I looked around, I didn't see any crop circles or mutilated cows.

A little more than 24 hours earlier, at five in the morning on October 3, I had stuck out my thumb on an entrance ramp to the I-5 in Eugene with a simple goal: to be in San Francisco by 7:00 p.m. The Grateful Dead were playing at the Warfield Theatre, and I had miraculously scored a ticket off the Student Exchange bulletin board at the University of Oregon.

At 21, I was young and foolish enough to think I could hitchhike to San Francisco, normally about a nine-hour drive from Eugene, and be on time. However, sometimes being young and a bit dim can work to your advantage: If I had honestly appraised my chances, logic would have dictated I stayed home. Leaving the day or night before wasn't an option; I had to work while in college. (Even with a job, I was still broke most of the time and what little money I had was spent on rent and Oregon's finest sinsemilla.)

There's always some poor soul headed to work at the ungodly hour of 5 a.m. and one such gentleman, an insurance salesman looking to break up the monotony of his morning routine, picked me up and drove me two exits south. I was on my way ! It was rare, in the days when it was safe to hitchhike in America, for a trucker to stop. Pulling an 18-wheeler onto a shoulder is dangerous. Fortunately, the traffic was light and, to my surprise, a truck pulled alongside the guardrail. I ran ahead and jumped into its cab.

The driver, a bearded, shaggy-haired man in his 30s, asked me where I was headed. "San Francisco," I replied, tossing my backpack onto the floor. "Well, then, today's your lucky day," he said, adding, "because that's exactly where I'm headed. Got a delivery to make on Fisherman's Wharf."

I told myself: *Coincidences like this aren't too common and usually better off not dissected too deeply.* This was, as a golfing friend once said after hitting a lucky shot, a case of "divine intervention." Eight hours later, we were driving into a fog-shrouded City by the Bay as the Bachman-Turner Overdrive hit, "You Ain't Seen Nothing Yet," ominously boomed about the cab. After having a slice of pizza on Market Street, I was in front of the Warfield at 5:00 p.m., or exactly 12 hours after I first stuck out my thumb.

And who's the first person I spy on the crowded street ?

Bill Graham.

I was in awe, standing alongside, to me, this mythological figure, rock's grandest promoter, a Holocaust survivor who, after World War II, landed in New York, where he lived in a foster-care home until being adopted by a Bronx family. After Bill graduated from DeWitt Clinton High School on Mosholu Parkway in the early 1950s, he was drafted and served in the Army. He faced court martial proceedings twice for minor infractions before winning both the Bronze Star and Purple Heart in combat duty during the Korean War.

I told Mr. Graham that I had grown up in the Bronx and had an uncle who graduated from Evander Childs High School on Gun Hill Road. He was very polite and genuine but before he would engage me, I could sense, he needed to ask me something: Did I have a ticket for tonight ?

Graham was, by all accounts, a straight shooter, a no-nonsense guy. What he was really asking was: *Do you have your act together or are you just another shuck-and-jiver with a clever introduction looking to scam me for a miracle ticket ?*

I showed him my ducat and he made me feel as if I had just presented an All Access laminate. He asked me about my uncle; I told him that he was a second baseman at Evander who was good enough to be offered a contract by the Yankees in the early 1920s. "But my great grandfather owned a barber shop in Westchester Square and his son was going to sweep hair until he learned how to cut it," I told Bill, adding, "instead, the Yankees signed some kid named Tony Lazzeri and the rest is baseball history."

He laughed. "Have you been to any of the other shows and seen the inside of the theatre yet ?" he asked. I told him no. Mr. Graham began to explain how he had adorned the theatre interior with posters and photographs from the Grateful Dead's history. We shook hands and he gave me a real firm shake, looking me square in the eye. That kind of eye contact can tell you all you need to know about what someone thinks, or doesn't think, of you.

My next goal — find a hit of acid — was easily accomplished: a hit of blotter, 100 mics, the seller assured me. I let the paper linger on my tongue as I strolled Market Street, watching the soft parade of Deadheads and hasty locals on their way home from work. Just before show time, certain I had purchased a bogus hit, I bought a second hit of LSD, a dose of Window Pane, guaranteed, I was told by its seller, to generate 150 mics of good times and lasting memories.

As I was about to enter the Warfield, Mr. Graham came over, tore my ticket, and led me through a side door. For the next five minutes, he became my personal tour guide: "And this picture is of me and Jerry backstage at the old Fillmore." "This photo was taken on the night I met Janis for the first time." "The bunting is from the closing of Winterland."

And then he was gone.

The Dead's acoustic set had a back-porch feel, highlighted by an instrumental "Heaven Help the Fool," Brent's harpsichord work on "China Doll," and the one song I was guaranteed to hear and was the most excited about — "Ripple." Making it even more ultra-cool: before playing the *American Beauty* track, Jerry, who rarely spoke onstage, offered, "Sing along with us if you like !"

The first electric set started strong, with a "Jack Straw", "Sugaree" opening salvo. The Dead were tight and on fire; the intimacy of the theatre and their closely-configured acoustic stage set-up was invigorating for them and Jerry. The music was sizzling, and the crowd heated. My 13th row seat gave me a mesmerizing, up-close view of the band. My only issue: I must have bought two bum hits of acid because I was not off and it was now well over an hour.

During "Row, Jimmy," a hulking, bearded Deadhead seated next to me passed me a joint stuffed with Humboldt's finest. One deep toke was all it took to light the fuse on the stick of dynamite that was 250 mics of LSD, which began to course through my central nervous system like white water rushing through rapids. *Oh, boy*. Like a rookie trying to score from second base on a single with one out in the ninth inning of a tied baseball game, this 21-year-old had run through a stop sign without even considering that, just maybe, not only would both hits be good but they would, in fact, be locally manufactured by well-intending, Owsley-inspired Deadhead chemists.

Who hasn't pulled that same bonehead maneuver before ?

As always seemed to be my fate, I started to peak during intermission. The walls were, once again, throbbing and the lights way too bright. Sheer torture. Fortunately, I remembered the photos on the walls and walked around the elegant lobby, looking at pictures of the Dead in Egypt, posters from the Avalon days, and photos of Bill Graham alongside everyone from Carlos Santana to Ronnie Van Zandt. I was rushing hard now, harder than Jim Brown carrying a football. I had experimented with mescaline and pushed the boundaries of my own fortune before but this was skirting the edges of reality.

As the houselights mercifully fell for the start of set three, I noticed it had become scorching hot inside. I saw Bill Graham open two balcony doors and step onto a fire escape. Silhouetted by streetlight, he stood there in solitude, unfazed by the music, staring into the night. It was past midnight and, hypothetically, exactly ten years to the moment Janis died. Meeting him seemed like an eternity ago. As the cool night air swept in, Jerry began to strum the opening chords to "Scarlet Begonias." I was way too high to be seated so close to the band; once again, my psychosis had kicked in: I was certain the Dead could tell I was tripping, so I abandoned my orchestra seat and made tracks for the balcony.

There, a pretty girl with long brown hair sat down next to me. I was dying to kick it with her but was battling a minor issue — the acid was torching my ass, my mind was all over the place, and I had entered, for me, uncharted territory, attempting to pull off a high-wire act I wasn't sure even Bronx street smarts could navigate. I decided to mention to her that I was really high and needed to chat when she turned to me and said, "I'm really high. Do you think we can talk ?"

I began to laugh and explained that I was about to ask her the same question, which made her break up. The levity, as it always seems to do during a "tripping crisis," had a grounding effect as Jerry sang, "The wind in the willows played 'Tea for Two.'"

Among the third-set highlights: Using telepathy to talk with Garcia amid an incendiary jam out of "Playing in the Band" (during which the guitarist told me "love is important") and a divine "Black Peter." Another: God explaining to me why I needed to disavow myself of worldly possessions. I got Garcia's message but took the word of the good Lord a bit too literally, leaving my billfold and its cash, tin of weed, backpack and baseball cap on my seat, which is how I woke up on the morning of October 4, 1980 in a field outside Eureka with no worldly possessions.

Two weeks later, a package arrived in the mail with my wallet and driver's license and a return address listed as Bill Graham Presents.

April 6, 1982

Driving south on the New Jersey Turnpike in a blinding snowstorm on the afternoon of April 6, 1982, smoking joint after joint, I watched with equal parts amusement and pity as one car after another skidded off the road, smacking into guardrails and each other, all the while wondering if tonight's Grateful Dead concert in Philadelphia would be canceled.

Remarkably, and thankfully, it wasn't. For the Dead, the ol' show business adage almost always held true:

The show must go on !

In front of the Spectrum on Broad Street, tickets were being given away; for once, it was the scalpers who were desperate and not us and that felt really good to me. Inside, the Spectrum, normally packed and electrified, was barely two-thirds full. The snow had kept everyone but only the most die-hard Deadheads and fans away and turned the massive coliseum into an intimate setting. I felt blessed to be there.

The emptier the house, it always seemed, the better the Grateful Dead played. Could it be they were insulted by the lack of a sellout, taking it personally and going about their business with giant chips on their shoulders ? Or perhaps the absence of a jammed arena lifted the considerable weight to excel every night off their backs, allowing them to feel at ease and perform effortlessly. Either way, the band was in a comfortable groove on the night of April 6, opening with an apropos "Cold Rain and Snow."

The Dead turned in a "we're in no hurry" 12-song first set. Twelve songs ! Included were an exquisite "Candyman" and beautifully-crafted versions of "Brown-Eyed Women" and Weir's "Looks Like Rain." A wicked "Shakedown Street" began set two, which I got a kick out of, as, due to the snow, there truly was "nothing shaking on shakedown street" ! Jerry followed with the opening chords of "Crazy Fingers" but remembered it was Bob's turn in the back-and-forth; Weir led the band through a sensational "Lost Sailor", "Saint of Circumstance." A magnificent, and grand, "Terrapin Station," with Jerry's voice sounding so young as I listen 35 years later, led into the drum solo.

The "space" segment was particularly captivating; Garcia's uncharted guitar forays into parts unknown synched nicely with the crazy thoughts running through my mind. A hard-fought "The Other One" featured only the second verse, leading into a monumental "Morning Dew." As Jerry sang and played, a hush, like April snow, fell over the audience. Mr. Garcia was on top of his game; the music may play the band, to paraphrase Barlow, but when Jerry was on (and he was on all night), he served as muse to the music.

Bob tore it up on "Sugar Magnolia," pulling out the full hambone act — bouncing the guitar off his knee, hopping toward the audience, snapping his head back and sending his hair flying. Assuming the pose of a victorious general, right arm held high, finger in the air, he signals to the band: It's a wrap.

Glory to the troops !

On this snowy evening, "It's All Over Now, Baby Blue" seemed like an appropriate nightcap.

Walking out of the Spectrum, built alongside the Vet (the Phillies' cookie-cutter baseball stadium), I quickly and cautiously strode through the parking lot. It was late, dark and sparsely populated. The pretzel sellers and factory tie dye hawkers were pissed off at the lack of customers.

I beat a path to my car. Philly is the last town you want to scuffle in; the hockey teams of the '70s, led by enforcer Dave Schultz, were nicknamed the Broad Street Bullies, an attitude upheld by the locals to this day.

Heading north through Jersey on a near-empty turnpike, a light snow still falling, I reveled in the after-show glow of the April 6 performance. I lit up one last joint, put on a tape of the Dead from the Carousel in '68, and ran one toll after another, a tramp like me, born to run.

April 8, 1982

The Grateful Dead annually pumped millions into the economies of northern and western New York towns such as Cortland, Glens Falls, Rochester, Buffalo, Niagara Falls, and so on.

For these towns, and towns across America, the Dead were the ultimate — and an instant — economic stimulus package. Everyone prospered when the caravan pulled into town: the 7-11s and Motel 6s; the concessionaires and ushers; the cops pulling OT; and the local bars, restaurants, pot dealers, mechanics and tow truck drivers. Unfortunately, area lawyers and town courts also made out well.

In the spring, upstate New York is breathtakingly beautiful, its countless towns defined by their geography, heritage and industry.

In early April, 1982, I took a solo road trip later dubbed "the War Memorial Tour" — back-to-back Grateful Dead shows at the Onondaga County War Memorial in Syracuse on April 8 and the Community War Memorial in Rochester the following night.

Before the Syracuse show, with the houselights still up, two curtains were slowly peeled back to reveal the Dead just standing there, Garcia with his guitar strapped on, his left hand around its neck, with no inclination toward tuning up or playing.

From each side of the stage, a group of war veterans wearing garrison caps proceeded to carry flags (one group held an American flag, the other a VFW flag) to center stage, near Weir's mic, where they slid each into a base. A scratchy recording of "The Star-Spangled Banner" began to play over the Dead's PA. Everyone, including the Deadheads, respectfully stood up. The band, and most of the audience, were as struck (and as bemused, in a non-condescending way) as I was by the simple yet dignified pageantry, a patriotic moment as American as baseball, apple pie and the Grateful Dead.

Everyone remained standing until the last notes faded and the only sounds were the crackles and pops of the vinyl. The vets returned the flags to each side of the stage as the houselights dimmed. The Dead finally began to tune up, eventually breaking into a "Feel Like a Stranger" opener as brisk as the upstate air.

June 10, 1984

Inside the Ken Kesey Archive in the Oregon library, where one of my journalism classes was held, I would freely rummage through boxes of Kesey's personal items and papers, including his hand-written notes for *One Flew Over the Cuckoo's Nest* and his second novel, *Sometimes a Great Notion* (1964).

Digging deeply, I uncovered, and blew the dust off, a hand-typed script for *Cuckoo's Nest* with actor Michael Douglas' name in ink on its cover. The script was intended for Douglas to read for the starring role of McMurphy, as his father, Kirk Douglas, owned the film rights and all the younger Douglas had to do was say "yes."

He passed.

The actor did, however, ask his dad to give a friend — a talented, aspiring actor who had been striking out in auditions because of his height — the career-altering role of Martini, the break Danny DeVito needed.

Kesey's first two books, *Cuckoo's Nest* and *Sometimes a Great Notion*, had established him as one of America's most-promising young writers. His acclaim grew after *Sometimes a Great Notion*, considered by many to be his finest work, was brought to the stage and then the Hollywood screen. The film adaptation of the novel — the 1971 movie *Never Give an Inch*, starring Paul Newman — garnered two Academy Award nominations and brought Kesey modest fanfare.

The 1975 film version of *Cuckoo's Nest* punched the author's ticket to the major leagues.

After class in the archive, I would Steve Prefontaine across the sprawling, fir-lined campus on my way to my Jackson Avenue home, the Eugene night bristling with the smells of pine, woodstoves and fireplaces.

March 29, 1985

On Shakedown Street, an innocuous and peaceful place for 'Heads to gather, incense and the sounds of Grateful Dead bootleg tapes filled the air. Your biggest concern was convincing your friends not to venture into the Krishna tent while tripping.

In 1985, I was 25 and about to start work as a first-year teacher in the South Bronx. Having seen the Grateful Dead with Keith and Donna Godchaux, I was given a certain revered status among my younger neighborhood Deadhead friends. I remember thinking: If this makes me cool, then what does that make the fans who saw the Dead with Pigpen !

Among those young Deadheads were my 18-year-old brother, Anthony, and his high school classmate, Jeffrey Reich, who had been begging me to take them to see the Dead. We picked out a Friday night — March 29, 1985 at the Nassau Coliseum on Long Island.

1985 was a great year to see the Grateful Dead. Onstage, they were cooking like Walter White in the Albuquerque desert.

On the afternoon of the 29th, I loaded Anthony, Jeffrey and a cooler of Tall Boys into my copper-colored '66 Chevy Caprice station wagon, replete with sideboards, simulated wood exterior trim, an overhead rack and a V8. I popped a cassette mix tape of Pink Floyd into the dash and lit up a joint, cruising south on the Bronx River Parkway as Floyd sang about the perils of education.

After crossing the city line, I steered the wagon onto the eastbound lanes of the Cross Bronx Expressway, the traffic flowing as freely as the beers, bones and 'shrooms. To our right, in the distance, the Empire State Building, the Chrysler Building and the World Trade Center glistened in the sun like golden beacons of Gomorrah. The cassette flipped over and "Us and Them" began to play. Abject poverty was all around us. The streets of the South Bronx were littered with the homeless, stray dogs, boarded-up bodegas and burned-out buildings, some still occupied.

Richard Wright's piano created a solemn environment inside the Caprice as I explained to Anthony and Jeffrey how, between 1957 and 1972, developer Robert Moses intentionally steered the Cross Bronx Expressway through the blue-collar heart of the Bronx — the Tremont and Soundview neighborhoods — to spare the Grand Concourse and its exquisite Art Deco apartment buildings, home to New York's most affluent and politically powerful. In doing so, Moses tore down homes, dynamited ridges and parkland, displaced countless businesses and decimated property values, ultimately creating what would come to be known as "the South Bronx."

As Floyd sang about "with and without," we quietly swigged beer, ate funky-tasting mushrooms, and stared at the destitution. The melancholy was broken when Jeffrey began to gag and almost barfed, but he managed to wash down the balled-up 'shrooms with a Tall Boy.

We were bound for Long Island, where the Grateful Dead were in town for a sold-out Friday night show. We didn't have tickets but that was not a concern. Despite the predicament in Binghamton five years ago, I wasn't concerned: We had a big bag of Jamaican weed and plenty of cash. Tickets were discreetly available, and we scored three for $75 and a handful of buds.

Last fair deal in the country.

"Cold Rain and Snow" was always one of my favorite openers — its upbeat introductory notes, the sincerity in Jerry's voice, and its woeful tale of love. Matt Kelly, on harmonica, joined the Dead for the Weir blues pairing of "Meet Me at the Bottom", "Ain't Superstitious." An ecliptic "Friend of the Devil" was followed by the first performance of "Supplication" in five years, which was thrilling to me, but when I tried to explain the significance to Anthony and Jeffrey, I might well have been trying to explain algorithms.

At halftime, as if he had been a Deadhead since the Fillmore East days, Anthony comically, and somewhat prophetically, commented, "I saw a bumper sticker earlier tonight in the parking lot that read: 'My other vehicle is a second set 'Terrapin.'"

Now, that is funny as hell, if you think about it.

I could tell Anthony and Jeffrey were having a blast. Who doesn't at their first Grateful Dead concert ? All the pretty ladies, the pot smoke that hangs in the air like pollen in April, the feeling that no one is judging you and, best, the realization that everyone is pretty much only concerned with having a good time. But I was hoping for an A-Ha Moment for the two, when everything becomes crystalline: On the surface, this may be a party but, beneath it all, there's something fascinating, unique and significant.

That moment came when Garcia strummed the opening notes to "Terrapin Station" to kick off the second set, a rare set opener. Endorphins, unchecked, raced through my body. As Jerry sang, "I will not forgive you if you will not take a chance," a single white spotlight silhouetted him, giving him a saintly aura. I looked at Anthony and Jeffrey. For the first time, the music had their full attention. They were listening and watching, looking on with the same awe and respect they showed when I took them to the Stadium to see Munson and Reggie play.

Jerry was masterful, holding court, drawing everyone in and encouraging us to ride the chicane with him. Occasionally, out of the corner of his eye, he looked over at the band, as if to let them know: I've gone for it tonight, boys, so buckle up. As the Dead reached the "Since the end is never told" refrain, Garcia was playing so fiercely that he was drawing primordial screams from the crowd. Weir had his palms in the air and was rocking to and fro as he sang, "He cannot be bought or sold …"

When I looked over, Anthony and Jeffrey were also holding their palms up, swaying in time like Bob. It was their moment, when the music, the lyrics, and the passion of the Deadheads all made it clear: There is something magical, mystical and magnificent about the Grateful Dead, intrinsic qualities that Anthony and Jeffrey can't quite grasp tonight, but I'm sure they'll figure it out soon enough.

November 21, 1986

John Barlow once told Jerry that he was considering going "out front" to frolic among the Deadheads in the parking lot. "I would, man, if I could," the guitarist wistfully told Barlow.

"He wanted to be with the Deadheads," John revealed to writer Robert Greenfield. "He said, 'I would, man, if I could. It looks a lot safer out there. But how would I know?'"

The Grateful Dead's video chief, Len Dell'Amico, recalled the time him and Garcia went to see Los Lobos in San Rafael on November 21, 1986, shortly after Jerry's recovery from a diabetic coma. "This was his first time out in public, and Mountain Girl made me promise to have him back after the early show," Len told *Rolling Stone*.

"Carlos Santana was there. They hadn't seen each other in years. Now, [we're] staying for the second set. In the middle of the second set, they called [Jerry] up onstage. They were doing 'La Bamba.' He was playing a guitar that he never held before, and he dropped in this incredible solo, and that was it. He was back.

"Then, it was two in the morning, and we couldn't find him anywhere. Finally, we walked out into the street, and there he was, waiting for us, talking to the fans one at a time. As I was driving home, he turned to me and said, 'You know, I haven't talked to these people in years.'

"It was like he didn't really remember how much they cared for him and had missed him."

It was both poignant and cathartic for Bob to sing "Miss You," a song from Phish's fantastic 2016 album, *Big Boat*, during his guest appearance with the Vermont quartet in Nashville on October 18, 2016.

Phish guitarist Trey Anastasio underwent a similar catharsis during the Dead's reunion shows in 2015 when he sang an emotional "Standing on the Moon," his voice cracking as he repeated the line "I'd rather be with you."

In April, 2009, Trey's sister, Kristy Manning (nee Anastasio), had passed away from cancer. That night in Chicago, she was clearly on his mind.

The music and lyrics to "Miss You" were penned by Trey to honor Kristy. The two were extremely close: from the beginning, she was highly supportive of her brother's decision to pursue a career in music and was also renowned as one of the first Phish fans.

"Miss You" is easily the most likeable, and accessible, tune on *Big Boat*. It's a show stopper and handing it off to Bob was a super classy move by Trey. The song is tailor-made for Weir to sing — it reaches soaring crescendos much in the same way "Looks Like Rain" does — and he absolutely nailed it, delivering "Miss You" with forcefulness and command. The same way Jerry made songs such as "I'll Take a Melody" and "Catfish John" sound as if he had penned them is the same way Bobby made everyone feel as if "Miss You" were written by him.

In fact, "Miss You" easily could have been written by Weir to address the sense of loss he endures over Garcia's passing:

There's a hole in my heart that will never be filled
This could all get easier but it never will
I float through the days and the long lonely nights

Later in the song, Trey writes:

In the faces of the people I see on the street
You're everywhere

Although Bob seems to have finally reached a place in his life where he has found peace — with himself, his family life, and his place in music history — he still sings of "one last river to cross" on his late-career masterstroke, *Blue Mountain*.

Is it possible Bobby sees the "last river to cross" as a reunion with Garcia in the next life ?

That's how I interpret it.

"My old pal, Jerry, had a place he used to talk about, a place of peace," he told *Rolling Stone*. "He described it as 'going down to the river.' After they cremated him ... I had a dream in which it was revealed that he wanted to go 'down to the river.'"

Mr. Weir took the dream to heart and scattered some of Jerry's ashes in the Ganges River in India. "I take my dreams quite seriously," he told the magazine.

Blue Mountain, and the subsequent support tours, served to re-affirm Bob's place atop the jamband and Grateful Dead worlds and his status as a vital voice in music today.

"One Last River to Cross" is simply Weir saying: "Garcia and I were too bonded in this life not to cross paths again."

And when that moment comes, after some small talk, the two will break out their guitars and get back to it.

Until then, as was the case with Trey when he sang "Standing on the Moon," for one night in Nashville, Phish allowed Bobby to use their music, and magic, to help him better come to terms with loss.

December 26, 1986

During the 1980s, Deadheads took advantage of the now-defunct but legendary airline PeoplExpress, which operated from 1981 to 1987 and was once the country's fifth largest air carrier, to see the Grateful Dead all over the country. If you have ever watched the 2004 comedy, *Soul Plane*, starring Tom Arnold and Snoop Dogg, then you have a basic understanding of what a flight aboard PeoplExpress could be like.

I loved the airline's name: PeoplExpress. It suggested something Communist: An airline run by the people, for the people. I half-expected to see an image of Chairman Mao or Leonid Brezhnev on the fuselage.

The rates were outrageously low. In 1986, flying from Newark, New Jersey to upstate New York (a home away from home for the Grateful Dead) cost $19 to Syracuse and $29 to Buffalo. In under two hours, you could be in Columbus, Ohio for just $49 and it was only $99 to fly to San Francisco !!

To fly on PeoplExpress, all you had to do, like booking a hotel room at the time, was call ahead and reserve a seat. No credit card required, no down payment necessary. My favorite part of flying on a PeoplExpress flight came when the stewardesses or stewards would start on opposite ends of the aisle and roll out — and I am not kidding — a cash register on wheels. They would head up and down the aisle, collecting fares paid by credit card, check or cash, before converging in the middle.

As the attendants worked their way down the center, the fun would really begin. It was not uncommon to see a 'Head take out a piggy bank, milk bottle or brown bag and pay for their fare in change: 116 quarters or 290 dimes got you from Newark to Buffalo ! On one memorable flight to Syracuse to see the Dead at the War Memorial in 1981, Deadhead after Deadhead began to disappear as the cash registers got closer and closer, packing themselves inside the bathrooms like college students in telephone booths during the Fifties. One or two contortionists even attempted to stuff themselves under their seats, and another tried the overhead compartment. It was madness with a touch of insanity and a dash of good ol' fun.

If the stewards did catch you in the bathroom or under a seat and you couldn't come up with the dough, you were in a heap of trouble: committing a crime on an airplane results in a federal charge. I would watch with sadness as the air marshals arrested Deadhead after broke Deadhead as they stepped onto the tarmac.

In 1986, smoking cigarettes was permissible on an airplane. Today, you would be arrested (if you were lucky) or violently dragged off the plane while being brow-beaten (if you weren't). Back then, smokers were seated in the rear but, unless you were in the cockpit, the smell would permeate the length of even a 747. It wasn't uncommon for people to enter the bathroom in the smoking section, take a few hits off a joint, exhale into the toilet as they flushed, and attempt to discreetly return to their seat. Occasionally, the odor would waif over the smoking section, leaving the perpetrator with a sheepish grin on his or her face.

On December 26, 1986, I flew PeoplExpress to San Francisco to catch the Grateful Dead's New Year's Eve run at the Henry J. Kaiser Auditorium in Oakland. The back section of the plane was slowly overrun by cigarette-smoking Deadheads, who, as we flew the friendly skies above the Midwest, became blatant, out-in-the-open pot-smoking Deadheads.

What could the good people of PeoplExpress, our hard-working comrades, do ? Because everything about the airline was cut-rate (you didn't even receive a bag of peanuts), there were just the two poor souls who collected fares and the two (I'm assuming there were two) pilots. How could four people stop an army of pot-smoking Deadheads ?

As the young 'Head seated next to me, a student from Amherst, Massachusetts. observed, "What they need is an airplane with windows that can be cracked to let out the smoke."

By the time that jet passed over the Rockies, pot smoking was going on in the back of the plane non-stop and unabated, as if the plane were, to be blunt (pun intended), the Soul Plane !

At first, I admit I was a little sanctimonious: Fucking Deadheads, acting up again. But by the time the airliner hit Salt Lake City, I too had my bag out, rolling up a fattie that would have made Willie Nelson proud. The attendants had long given up, and the passengers seated up front had accepted their strange reality. Someone took out a small boombox and put on a Dead bootleg. It was utter chaos and total lawlessness; the only thing missing was a vat of Kool-Aid.

The marshals were waiting as we came down the exit ramp. Only this time, inside of behaving surly and acting aggressively, they looked flustered and perplexed. As the Deadhead from Amherst walked past me, I heard him cynically remark under his breath, "You can't arrest all of us !"

December 28, 1986

Deep inside the Kaiser Auditorium, the first live streaming of a Grateful Dead concert took place on December 28, 1986 — the second show of the Dead's four-night stand at the Kaiser Auditorium in Oakland. How could such an event have occurred a decade or so before the Internet existed and long before the vision and technology needed for live music streaming ?

As the houselights lowered and the band strolled onstage, I noticed a payphone attached to a support column in the vestibule, less than 50 feet from the stage. I buried a handful of quarters into its coin slot and called my friend Terence Hanrahan in Manhattan; he had just started a new telecommunications job and I wanted to see how his first week went. I was hoping to keep it brief, as I didn't want to come across as "out here in Oakland, partying" while Ter was back home in New York going through the grind, and trials and tribulations, of a new job.

Terence excitedly began to tell me about his new gig as the band warmed up in the background; before I could say goodbye, Jerry rifled the opening notes of "Cold Rain and Snow." I felt terrible. Terry loved the Dead as much as anyone, and I had hoped our conversation would be over before the band began to play, as I figured the sound of the music, even a brief snippet through a tiny speaker, would be exciting to him at first but then disheartening once I ran out of quarters.

"Scott," he told me on the other end, excitement in his voice, "I can hear it as clear as day."

I was thrilled but told Terence I only had two quarters left — about another ten minutes of time — before the line would go dead.

Why didn't Terence just call me back ? Calling across the United States, even at night, wasn't cheap in 1986. There was no such thing as cell phones or unlimited minutes or even a choice of carriers; in New York, you used Bell Telephone or a string and a cup. As Weir led the band into "Minglewood Blues," I deposited my final .25 cent piece. I asked Terry how the job went. "Great," he told me. "Good starting salary, benefits, company car, a calling card."

Did he just say "calling card " ?

Thirty years ago, a corporate calling card was the equivalent of a corporate expense account today, a great perk that you could use to save on your own phone bill. You dialed or punched "O," gave the operator the number you wanted to reach, and simply read off the seven digits on the card.

"Give me the number on the payphone," Terence instructed.

I knew what he was up to.

"My boss told me I get 35 hours of phone time a month with this card. Stay right there, I'm gonna try to call you right back."

Jerry strummed the opening chords to "Row, Jimmy" as Terence hung up.

A short time later, the phone rang. It startled a few of the hallway dancers and twirlers; who expects to hear a ringing phone during a red-hot "Stagger Lee" ?

"Hello ?" I answered, acting as if I had no idea who might be on the other end.

I have always loved Terence; he remains a best friend and I treasure the anarchic streak we both share — the willingness, as he would put it, to push the envelope. "Scottie," he excitedly told me, "I got the whole thing up and running."

He detailed how he had unscrewed the top off his phone's receiver, wired a thing-a-ma-jiggy into the receiver and patched a line out of the thing-a-ma-jiggy into his stereo, which featured two six-foot JBL speakers. Or, as Terence would later explain: "Copper wire analog carried a good audio signal from what-was-then a new-ish public phone handset. On my side of the country, I had a land-line phone with an audio pick-up recorder connected via 9-pin DIN to the back of my Pioneer receiver using the Mono button and … *voilà* ! I was able to record onto a cassette in real time with no phone bill to pay !"

He quietly told me, "I can't make it too loud, it's 11 o'clock and a Sunday night, I don't want to wake the neighbors. But you should hear this. With the lights down low, a glass of wine and a few hits off a joint, I am right there with you."

I gently placed the phone handle atop the payphone, the speaker and earpiece pointed up, like a puppy lying on its back. The crowd broke into the "We want Phil !" chant and the bassist came to the mic and said something that sounded like, "Just ask for it." His voice was distorted by soundman Dan Healy, who put reverb on it from behind the soundboard.

Mr. Lesh delivered a kicking "Box of Rain." Jerry played with a lot of twang in his guitar, and Phil elicited a big cheer when he sang, "What do you want me to do, to watch for y'all while y'all sleeping." I had never heard Phil use the term "y'all" before (Bobby, yes), or since, not that there's anything there worth reading into, other than the effect it had on Terence some 3,200 miles to the east. Like Old Faithful bursting from Yellowstone's hallowed ground, I could feel the excitement pulsating from the phone. The Dead went up-tempo, with "Big Railroad Blues" and a set-closing "Promised Land."

I dashed to the phone before the house lights rose. "You still there ?"

"Not only am I here, I'm recording this and will have a copy to you in the mail by tomorrow afternoon," came the voice on the other end. "I just placed a pinch of mushrooms between my cheek and gum and plan on taking this deep into the night with you."

"I'm gonna buy a few beers and get a coupla more quarters," I replied. "Let me hang up in case someone needs to use the phone. I'll call you back as soon as I see the Dead walk back out."

I'm not sure why, but just before the second set began, Phil came to the mic and said, "Well, I guess we can't fool you guys !" His remark drew another huge cheer from the crowd just as the phone unexpectedly, and loudly, rang. Out of nowhere, Bill Graham suddenly appeared, casting a suspicious eye my way, like a teacher who thinks you're up to no good during an exam. The phone rang a second time. Mr. Graham stared at me, curious to see what I would do. With a "Can you believe that ?" look on my face, I causally picked it up, remarking to the promoter, "Probably some kid's mother looking to check up on him."

Mr. Graham smiled and kept moving.

Whew.

That fooled him.

Terry was on the other end: "I got this fine-tuned, the treble and bass perfect. If I didn't know better, I'd swear I'm right there with you inside the Kaiser."

I laid the receiver back down. Jerry was leading the band into "Scarlet Begonias" and I had no choice but to dance. The Grateful Dead were playing with an amazing on-stage dynamic, as Brent had long become a seamless part of their live chemistry. On this cold, wintry night, no one could know, or even suspect, the Dead were just months away from the career-altering success of *In the Dark* and "A Touch of Grey." As great as they were this evening, it would hardly compare to the confident, masterful band they would become in 1988 and '89, the result of their empowering commercial successes of 1987.

Occasionally, a curious 'Head would pick up the phone to see if anyone was on the other end. On Terence's tapes, you can hear him gleefully talking with random people, explaining to one cheery soul after another that he was in New York listening to the show live. Deadheads were so polite: "Oh, my God, that's so awesome ! Let me put the phone back down." To a person, they thought it was as cool as a drive down Lombard Street with Neal Cassady at the wheel.

"He's Gone" paired the beautiful timbre of Garcia's voice with Brent's melodic electric piano and vocals. Brent and Jerry worked well together onstage, like a perfectly-blended cup of morning coffee. A soaring "Black Peter," a song Robert Hunter once described as "a real monster," brought everyone, and the show, to a peak.

Would the post-*In the Dark* world of the Grateful Dead been different if the ticketless crowds that destroyed the scene outside stadiums and arenas had stayed home because they had the option to tune in to a live stream ? Not likely, as most of the problems were caused by people with little to no connection to the Deadhead scene and our core values and principles.

Three decades of perspective has taught me this: There's no way Bill Graham didn't know what I was up to ! You don't fool someone from the Bronx that easily. I seriously doubt I was the first Deadhead he caught calling a friend at home and leaving the receiver off the hook. That said, if you knew Bill, they say, he was a great guy.

Every December 28, Terry and I talk about that magical night, and the fun of it, and we both say the same thing: "I just listened to the tapes and they still sound amazing."

Summer, 1987

Bob Bralove, who joined the Grateful Dead's sound crew in 1987, shared this wonderful Brent anecdote.

Among his many duties and accomplishments, Mr. Bralove handled the routing of the Musical Instrument Digital Interface (MIDI) system onstage and, with Dan Healy, installed the technology in every Grateful Dead member's equipment between 1987 and 1989. Brent, who was first to have MIDI wired into his keyboard rig, then taught the rest of the Dead how the system worked.

"I had spent the summer (of 1987) working with the band on the Dylan-Dead tour, bringing all the sounds I had developed in the studio with them to their live performances," recalls Bralove. "That was the test tour to see if I could handle the scene and to see if the scene could handle me.

"After that tour, I was hired as a full-time employee. At my first gig as a full-time insider, Brent walks up to me and says, 'So, you decided to take the gig.'

"I responded, 'Hell, yes' with a smile. Then Brent said, 'Good, *now you're the new guy !*'"

SET ONE

December 4 and 5, 1987

Jerry admired brilliant people, among them bluegrass legends, cartoonists, authors, film directors and pro athletes.

The Grateful Dead guitarist made no secret of his admiration for artist Will Elder (in one of his last interviews, he praised Elder and the early *MAD* magazine artists), writer Kurt Vonnegut (Jerry owned the film rights to *The Sirens of Titan*), and directors Orson Welles, Francis Ford Coppola, James Whale and Wojciech Has.

He dug Joe Montana, Jerry Rice and Willie "The Say Hey Kid" Mays and was in awe of bluegrass stalwarts LeRoy Mack, Del McCoury and Bill Monroe, whom he met as a youngster and stood gap-jawed next to.

On the nights of December 4 and 5, 1987 at the Wiltern Theatre in Los Angeles, Jerry hosted one of his icons, LeRoy Mack, providing the renowned dobro and lap steel guitar player and his son with backstage passes and orchestra seats.

Jerry was performing in L.A. with the Jerry Garcia Acoustic Band and knew Mr. Mack lived locally. According to his website, Mack is a Southern California native who "has been playing bluegrass music for over fifty years. The bluegrass bug bit after hearing a Flatt and Scruggs record; LeRoy became acquainted with a Southern California group playing bluegrass called the Country Boys (later called the Kentucky Colonels)."

The band was in search of a dobro player and invited Mack to join them; he played with the Kentucky Colonels for four years, appearing on several LPs and both local and network television shows, most notably "The Andy Griffith Show."

Garcia loved the Kentucky Colonels.

Jerry hosted another of his idols, bluegrass maven Del McCoury, who brought along a couple of banjos to the backstage area of the Cap Center in Landover in 1991. McCoury first came to renown in 1963 as a guitarist and singer with Bill Monroe.

Garcia and McCoury most likely exchanged a Bill Monroe tale or two. In the summer of 1964, Jerry and Sandy Rothman, according to Rothman, "hung out for weeks" at Bill Monroe's Brown County Jamboree, a country music park about twenty miles outside Bloomington, Indiana. Rothman, a heralded mandolin, dobro and banjo player and member of the Garcia Acoustic Band, would go on to play with both the Kentucky Colonels and, ironically, Bill Monroe. Recalling the summer of '64, Rothman reminisces, "One weekend, Monroe was playing at the park and I asked Neil [Rosenberg, who managed the park], if he would introduce us to Monroe. He said, 'Just talk to him yourselves.' Garcia and I were not ten feet from where Monroe was and we didn't know what to say to him."

There are two interesting things about photos of Jerry standing alongside the people he looked up to: how happy he was next to the likes of Mr. Mack, Eric Clapton or Will Elder, and how his idols appeared to be equally honored !

On his website, LeRoy Mack would later proudly post the tickets, passes and a hand-written setlist he was given by Jerry.

September 24, 1988

The thing I remember best about the evening of September 24, 1988 was that my brother Chris and I gave Jerry a good laugh.

The Grateful Dead's historic nine-night residency at Madison Square Garden in September, 1988 culminated with a show on the 24th — the final night of the run — that benefited the green organizations Rainforest Action Network, Cultural Survival, and Greenpeace.

For the September 24 show, GDTS sold "Circle of Gold" tickets at $250 apiece that provided concert-goers with orchestra seats and passes to an after-show party at a Soho loft.

Weeks earlier, I had sent in my mail-order request and anxiously awaited its arrival. When the envelope turned up inside my mailbox in mid-August, I skipped the elevator and, with great anticipation and excitement, ran up six flights, opened the door to my Inwood apartment, rolled a zeppelin, and fired it up.

Chris and I caught our first show at the Garden on Thanksgiving night, 1974 — the historic Elton John concert that became John Lennon's final public performance. The Garden's floor plan was seared into our young minds. In the '70s, tickets for the orchestra were brown (representing the Earth) while the seats from the loge on up were laid out in the color scheme of a rainbow. The loge was red, the 100 section was orange, the 200s were yellow, the 300s green, and the rafters, or 400 section, home to blue-collar, die-hard Knicks and Rangers fans, were, appropriately, blue.

Orchestra seating was arranged by a letter system: the front four sections were O - R - A - C. As we learned the hard way, you did not want to sit in sections O or C, as that meant getting throttled by the Marshall stacks on each side of the stage. After sitting in section O, row 5 for a 1976 double-bill that featured Aerosmith opening for Black Sabbath, it took three weeks for the ringing to disappear from my 17-year-old ears.

I drew deeply on the joint and slowly opened the GDTS envelope. Out tumbled two tickets in Section A, row 1, seats 1 and 2. I had to put down the doob and look several times to convince myself that we had been gifted the two best seats in the house from the kind folks at GDTS.

Woo hoo !

Arena officials had allowed the Dead to fasten an inflatable King Kong in a tie-dyed T-shirt atop the famed marquee on Seventh Avenue. After soaking in the street fair, we entered the Garden, where we were treated like rock royalty. An usher outfitted in a red-and-black uniform wearing a red cap with gold piping and a black brim led us to our seats. As I slipped him a five, he asked if we were Atlantic Records' co-founder Ahmet Ertegun's grandkids.

Jerry seemed thrilled to be playing with artists as diverse as Suzanne Vega and Hall and Oates. The show had some great moments — one was a guest spot from Mick Taylor, formerly of the Rolling Stones, on slide guitar during "Little Red Rooster." When Hall and Oates strode onstage, Garcia was all smiles as he strummed the opening chords to Marvin Gaye's "What's Going On," written by Gaye after the Motown superstar witnessed police brutality at an anti-Vietnam War rally in Berkeley.

The nine nights turned out to be one of the Grateful Dead's greatest residencies anywhere, ever; the energy levels were sky-high and the playing sharp and crisp. Ovations swept down from the blue section to the front rows of O-R-A-C following killer show-ending versions of "Morning Dew" on the 14th and 20th.

After the "Good Lovin'", "Knocking on Heaven's Door" encore, featuring the full ensemble of performers, including the venerable Jack Casady, Chris and I hailed a cab and beat it on down the line to Alphabet City, where we soon found, and entered, a tiny loft, beautifully adorned in exotic tapestries and draperies and softly lit with pastel colors. Incense filled the air and burning candles added to the alluring ambiance. As you entered, you were given a graphic-design poster by the heralded American painter and artist Robert Rauschenberg.

A procession of percussionists and dancers, led by Mickey, Billy and Baba Olatunji, greeted us. I can still see the exuberance in Billy's eyes as the parade snaked around the room, disappearing down a corridor just as Brent walked in. I introduced myself and shook his hand. We chatted about how neat it was to see his daughter sit next to him on his piano bench earlier in the week during "I Will Take You Home." I asked Brent to sign my Rauschenberg poster and he gladly complied. He was polite and friendly but exhausted, literally still sweaty. He excused himself and headed off to say hello to some friends.

The wine and beer were flowing and Deadheads, myself among them, were very excited. A few discreetly lit up joints as waiters walked around with trays of vegetarian fare. My brother and I sat at a table with a host of other 'Heads, chowing down and chatting about the show.

Chris ran into Bill the Drummer and he signed his poster. As we ate, fans began to line up in front of two tables where Bobby and Jerry were seated. We took our place on line, posters in hand. Not a moment later, a burly security guard drew a velvet rope behind us and loudly declared no one else would be allowed on line, which is when Chris realized he had left his camera on the table.

Assuming the security guard would be amenable, he jumped off the line, ran back to the table, and retrieved the Kodak. When he attempted to re-take his place, the guard refused to allow him entrance. Just a few feet from Garcia, we got to jawing. Our heavy Bronx accents caught Jerry's attention, and he began to watch the brewing rhubarb with the bemused look of a child enjoying a Saturday morning cartoon. The gruff man wouldn't back down and a fracas was about to break out.

Gesturing with his hands, Chris loudly declared, "Jerry, this guy ain't being cool." To his credit, Garcia didn't turn his head or pretend he wasn't aware of what was going on. Some other "rock star" might have looked away but, in his squeaky voice, he told the guard, "Hey, man, let him through."

Who says "No" to the great Jerry Garcia ?

Certainly not Mr. Pinkerton.

And then Garcia let loose a chuckle, smiling as he shook his head at our Beavis and Butthead-like antics. "C'mon over," he offered.

Jerry was very polite and friendly — looked you in the eye. He asked us where we were from and when I told him the Bronx, he laughed again, as if our near-brawl now made sense.

He was tired. There were women and hangers-on all over him and he was genuinely bothered by them. I simply thanked him for the music and the effort. He was gracious as he listened to our compliments, signing, in his chaotic up-and-down hand-writing, our Rauschenberg posters. We shook his big mitt before walking over to Weir, sporting a ponytail, as was all the rage in 1988. Bobby was equally polite and friendly. I told him that I was a writer for *Relix* who had been giving a lot of ink to organizations such as Greenpeace in my "Fragments" column. He thanked me, signed our posters, and shook our hands.

As Chris and I turned to leave, we looked back at Jerry. Someone was whispering in his ear and he looked bothered again.

July 7, 1989

As a performing band, the Grateful Dead, like a business, had a career arc. The Dead's business was music, they made a career out of selling their transformational concerts as a way for Deadheads and music fans alike to rise above the day-to-day ho hum of life, and business was always brisk.

On July 7, 1989 at JFK Stadium in Philadelphia, the Grateful Dead's twelve-minute take on "Blow Away" has become the peak of their performing career — the band at its absolute in-concert zenith, the pinnacle of their performing prowess, the height of their live career arc.

Brent is fully in charge as Garcia gleefully works a glass slide up and down the neck of Tiger. His long-time sidekick, Weir, is a bystander, free of the rock star persona, able to focus on creating rhythms as, in my opinion, the greatest rhythm guitarist in rock history. Big Steve Parish can be seen intently looking on from the shadows, in case anyone has any foolish stage-crashing ambitions.

Hart and Kreutzmann beat as one heart while Phil is running his fingers all over the fretboard of his six-string bass with the abandon of newlyweds on their honeymoon night.

The sea of fans is stunning. The stadium is packed to the last row. The ancient JFK had multiples gates and conniving or sneaking into the venue was not a problem. Crowd estimates for the show have numbered as high as 100,000. The Dead's filled-to-the-brim gig turned out to be the last event at historic JFK, which was later torn down.

Wielding Pigpen-like power, Brent works each and every person among the 100,000 with the command of a Baptist preacher on Sunday morning. It was still daylight and only the first set but this 12-minute performance of "Blow Away" captures, and encapsulates, the best of the Grateful Dead from any era. The band plays with total confidence and masterful musicianship; the Core Five serve as happy-to-excel-in-the-background musicians. The Deadheads and fans pour their hearts out to, and energies into, the band.

For twelve glorious minutes on a scorching afternoon in Philly during the summer of 1989, the Dead hit the high-water mark of their live career with 100,000 witnesses attending the sermon, all of whom will testify that this was the only universe that was real and the only world that mattered.

SET ONE

October 9, 1989

There are "firsts" we never forget: our first kiss, major league baseball game, Broadway play or sexual encounter.

As Deadheads, there are also firsts we will never forget: our first Grateful Dead concert, the first time we tripped at a Dead show, the first time you heard the Dead (or, for younger or newer 'Heads, one of their off-shoot bands) play "Morning Dew," "St. Stephen" or "Dark Star." For me, those were, and remain, the Big Three, the Holy Trifecta of the live canon.

I caught my first "Dew" at Nassau in March, 1980 and was blessed to be at the Garden on October 11, 1983 when the band returned "St. Stephen" to the rotation for the first of three performances that fall, which turned out to be the last three times the Dead played the *Aoxomoxoa* haymaker.

But "Dark Star" ?

No luck.

I had several near-misses: they played the Hunter-Garcia aria the night before my first show; there was an unrelenting "Dark Star" on New Year's Eve 1981, or a year before I began seeing the band's New Year's runs. In the summer of 1984, I thought about, but passed on, flying out to Berkeley for the annual Greek Theatre shows. On July 13 at the Greek, a shooting star passed across the night sky moments before the Dead broke into "Dark Star."

Like the shooting star, I was beginning to believe my opportunity had come and gone.

As if competing in the 24 Hours of Le Mans, the journey had become an endurance test as much as a quest. The odyssey led me and a group of close friends from George Washington University, all in search of our first "Dark Star," south on I-95 to the Mother Ship also known as the Hampton Coliseum.

By performing two gigs under the pseudonym "Formerly the Warlocks" and only selling tickets locally and regionally, a lot of the pressure the band was constantly being put under by the parking lot scene was eliminated. There was less craziness than usual outside, the Dead were relaxed, and, in late '89, at the pinnacle of their performing prowess. The band was clicking on all cylinders and Jerry's playing could charm the birds out of the trees, as they say in Iowa.

Garcia was playing Wolf, which he had taken out of retirement, as Bob Bralove had recently outfitted it with MIDI. With the new technology and his old friend, Wolf, Garcia was a kid in a toy shop.

The Hampton shows featured a number of rare jewels. On the 8th, after a hiatus, the Dead broke out "Help on the Way", "Slipknot !" and encored with "And We Bid You Goodnight," which they had just returned to the rotation in July.

It seemed the entire song catalog was in play.

On the 9th, the air was heavy with anticipation. The second set began with a stellar "Playing in the Band",

"Uncle John's Band", "Playing in the Band" reprise. Garcia and Weir crossed up the verses a few times in "Uncle John's Band" but everyone just smiled. Using the MIDI, Jerry blew several lengthy flute solos during the post-"Playing in the Band" passage and the "Uncle John's Band" that followed.

Coming out of the "Playing" reprise jam, Jerry, almost inaudibly, hit the first two or three notes to "Dark Star," as if to cue the group. It was nearly impossible for me to fathom the possibility. Sure enough, Garcia stepped forward and picked the song's familiar opening notes. It took an equally-stunned audience a full three seconds before they exploded in joy, such was everyone's disbelief. My friends and I huddled together, hugging as if we had just won the Super Bowl.

Jerry had a sly look on his face. He knew how important this was to us, even if it was just another day at the office for him. To our utter joy, the Dead performed a transcendent, and lengthy, "Dark Star," an amazing moment in my life as a Deadhead.

The encore ?

The first performance of "Attics of My Life" since 1972.

For two nights inside the Hampton transporter, the scene outside had returned to the "free ticket for a hug" days, the bad people stayed away, and the band let down their hair.

All the way down.

1990

Rosebud — one of Jerry's final primary on-stage guitars (along with the Stephen Cripe-built Lightning Bolt) — was originally known as "the Saint."

And the story behind the original name is quite interesting. To guard Garcia, Doug Irwin intentionally choose an inlay of a protective saint in the act of warding off death.

A close inspection of Rosebud's inlay reveals a skeleton wearing a skirt holding both a rose and an ankh pendant (the ankh is an ancient Egyptian symbol for life) on a necklace in its right hand while its left hand is upright and is making the Sign of the Horns.

A rotation of more than a half-dozen of Jerry's guitars — including Rosebud — were displayed at the Rock and Roll Hall of Fame + Museum as part of a retrospective titled "Grateful Dead: The Long, Strange Trip," which ran from April, 2012 through March, 2013.

Little more than a decade earlier, the idea of having a collection of Garcia's guitars in the same room at the same time was as far-flung as the notion of Leicester City winning the EPL crown in 2016.

In 2001, a divisive issue rose among the Core Four as a result of Jerry's will: Weir, Kreutzmann, Hart and Grateful Dead Productions contested the will, arguing that two guitars — Wolf and Tiger (both bequeathed by Garcia to Irwin) — were the Dead's property, since GDP had paid for them.

After Phil publicly sided with Irwin, the matter had to be resolved in court. As per the terms of the settlement, the Dead's organization received Rosebud while Wolf and Tiger were awarded to Irwin, who auctioned them in 2002 to finance a guitar workshop and pay hospital bills.

During an auction on May 8, 2002 at former Manhattan hotspot Studio 54, Tiger sold (with commissions) to Indianapolis Colts' owner Jim Irsay for $957,500, making his winning bid $850,000. Wolf sold to Hyatt-family heir and Sonia Dada band member Dan Pritzker for $789,500 (making his winning bid $700,000).

The combined sale of $1.74 million set an auction record.

The rotation of Jerry's guitars at the Rock and Roll Hall of Fame + Museum exhibition included Rosebud; Tiger, on loan from Irsay; Wolf, on loan from Pritzker; two Stephen Cripe-designed guitars (Lightning Bolt and a second six-string known as Top Hat), and one of the Travis Bean guitars.

In 2009, the reclusive Mr. Irwin explained in a rare interview (with dozin.com) why his intended name for Rosebud was the Saint: "It has the skeleton saint on it ... the skeleton saint in the act of repelling death."

Irwin never attempted to pitch the Saint moniker to Garcia.

Rosebud was built, says Irwin, with "the same materials as the Tiger ... it's kind of a duplicative of it, although it's not quite as ornate as the Tiger."

In 2014, *Guitar Aficionado* declared: "Garcia considered [Rosebud to be Irwin's] masterpiece. Rosebud was similar to Tiger, but it featured three humbucking pickups, a Roland GK-2 hexaphonic guitar synthesizer pickup with its MIDI and synth controls internally mounted, and hollow body cavities that reduced the overall weight by two pounds."

Mr. Irwin would eventually build a fifth guitar for Jerry — which the luthier dubbed Wolf Jr. — but, according to Irwin, Wolf Jr. was "the one [Garcia] never really used much onstage or anything. It's a guitar that doesn't have a head because it has a really unusual tremolo system on it. It's a Steinberger Trans Trem, and it uses strings, it has a ball end on each end of the string. So, it didn't have a peghead on it."

Despite the falling out over the Irwin guitars, the past 20-plus years ultimately brought both rebirth and redemption for the remaining members of the Grateful Dead.

The road, as demonstrated by the acrimony over Garcia's guitars, wasn't always easy.

July 26, 1990

Just as there are some Deadheads who believe the Grateful Dead were never the same after Pigpen passed away, there are also many who feel the Dead were never the same after Brent's untimely passing in 1990.

One of the band's most-beloved members, Brent has, deservedly, taken on an iconic stature in Grateful Dead history.

Sadly, and tragically, as Brent took command of the Grateful Dead, he simultaneously, and unimaginably, lost control of his personal life. One day you're the keyboard player in Silver, opening for the Doobie Brothers in Smalltown, USA before a crowd of 5,000, the next day you're in front a packed football stadium with 60,000 adoring fans, the new star of the Grateful Dead.

How many 30-year-olds are going to handle that well ?

"Baby Boomer" Deadheads who celebrated their peak years seeing the Grateful Dead in the 1980s got to watch Brent grow into his role with the band. With each passing show and year, it became clear he was a prodigiously-talented musician. Brent pulled off the daunting task of a near-seamless assimilation into the Dead while making their music his music, the same way Ronnie Wood has been able to make the Rolling Stones' music his music.

Best, the keyboardist bonded with Jerry onstage, invigorating him, and, as the years passed, sharing a musical conversation with the guitarist, the band and us. As Deadheads, we were blessed to be able to participate in that repartee.

Like the Hawks (later the Band), who cut their teeth backing Ronnie Hawkins, the Grateful Dead made one heck of a backing band, whether it was for Bo Diddley, Spencer Davis or Suzanne Vega, or for Bob Dylan, John Fogerty or Stephen Stills.

When it came time for the Dead to become Brent's support unit, they were thrilled to give him all the room he needed.

Jerry, more than anyone in the Dead, was most contented as a sideman.

The shadows served Garcia well.

In the spotlight, Mydland belted out showstoppers such as "Blow Away," "Don't Need Love" and "The Devil in the Blue Dress" medley. Like Pigpen, Brent worked the Hammond B-3 with authority.

After Brent's sad death at age 37, Garcia was so wounded he insisted the B-3 be retired. It was also the first time he considered leaving the Grateful Dead, telling Manasha Matheson that, if she asked, he would ditch the band to focus on their family life. (She couldn't.)

The peak of the Brent era — 1988 through the summer of 1990 — is one of the most-solvent live periods in the Grateful Dead's performing history and the one I remember best.

Fall, 1990

Although they never met in person, the lives of Jerry Garcia and pioneer gangsta rap artist Tupac Shakur intersected in a manner that Jerry may, or may not, have been aware of. Shakur, however, was more than aware of who Jerry was and his storied place in music, culture and history.

In 1990, Shakur and his posse got seriously loose during a wild party thrown by Garcia's daughter, Trixie, inside the guitarist's Marin digs while the Grateful Dead were on the road.

Trixie was closely-guarded about her personal life and Shakur only realized who her father was after seeing Jerry on the cover of a magazine and making the connection. The rapper was tight with Trixie, who had this to say about Shakur in a 2014 interview with talk show host Pete Holmes: "He was the only friend of mine ... who even had any reverence for my dad or appreciation of him."

Tupac was born in 1971 and raised by two parents who were card-carrying members of the Black Panther Party in the late 1960s and early 1970s, which informed his music, lyrics and life code.

Shakur's father, Billy Garland, was an active member of the Black Panthers, his godfather was a high-ranking Panther, and his stepfather, Mutulu Shakur, was on the FBI's Ten Most Wanted Fugitives list from 1982-86.

His mom, Afeni Shakur, spent the first eight months of her pregnancy with Tupac in prison, facing 150 counts of "conspiracy against the United States government and New York landmarks" in the New York Panther 21 trial. While in jail, Afeni read *History Will Absolve Me* by Fidel Castro and successfully defended herself in the Panther 21 trial, getting acquitted on all counts. She was released from prison in May, 1971 and, a month later, her son was born on June 16.

Growing up in East Harlem, Shakur was educated by his parents about the community social programs and health clinics overseen by the Black Panthers in Oakland and across the nation during the mid-to-late 1960s as well as the armed patrols that followed police officers on duty in the Bay Area in 1967. He was also taught about the militant, hard-core principles and values of the Black Panthers and the Black Liberation Army by his extremist mom and her friends, nearly all of whom had served jail time for offenses committed as members of the Black Panthers, charges they were later largely acquitted of.

His upbringing played a major role in establishing the ethos of gangsta rap.

The Shakurs recognized they owed it to their three children to remove them from the violent world of New York City and to provide each with the opportunity to grow up in a civilized society that was not ruled by guns, gangs, hard drugs, death and hopelessness.

On New Year's Eve 1981, Jerry married his second wife, Carolyn Adams ("Mountain Girl"), backstage at the Oakland Coliseum between sets of the Grateful Dead's annual gala. Garcia and Adams had been living together in Marin County, where they were raising three daughters.

In 1988, the Shakur family went in search of a community with a safe environment, a good school system, and a reputation for intellectualism and heady idealism.

The Shakurs relocated to Mill Valley in Marin County, where Tupac attended Tamalpais High School. Free of the overwhelming despair of New York City, he flourished as a student, performing in school plays and excelling in English composition while also attending classes by poet Leila Steinberg in Oakland. Ms. Steinberg had a gift for working with at-risk students and became a mentor to Tupac and, later, his first manager.

At Tamalpais, Tupac made a new friend, a younger student who could relate to his penchant for real and actual revolution, as her dad possessed the same anarchistic streak: Trixie Garcia, the youngest of Jerry and Adams' girls. Trixie became good friends with Tupac and his buddies, dating Teron Jones, the Oakland rapper known as Del the Funkyhomosapien.

In the fall of 1990, while the Grateful Dead were touring, 16-year-old Trixie held a party at her dad's home (Jerry and Adams split in 1986), inviting Tupac and his crew. Trixie talked about the night during an "Ask Me Anything" discussion on Reddit.com on June 27, 2017: "Yes, Tupac came over to Jerry's house when Jerry was on the road. They didn't destroy it, but I have a distinct memory of people handing keyboards through the windows.

"Let me clarify. Tupac certainly wasn't a thief and his friends weren't thieves. It was a party that got out of hand. It was my good relationship with Tupac and his boys in Marin City that allowed me to get all that stuff back.

"And Jerry never noticed. Or Jerry might have noticed but he was such a non-confrontational kind of dad that he never told me that he noticed."

Garcia had his own set of anarchistic values with his principle belief being: No one has the right to tell another person how to live. So much so that he refused to sign any of the letters distributed by the Grateful Dead organization in the late 1980s and early 1990s that offered guidelines and suggestions for improved fan behavior inside and outside Dead concerts.

That might seem inconsequential or trite to some, but, to me, it speaks to a very rigid, and highly singular, life code.

Like Jerry, Tupac would establish his own code, set in stone, in the words of one writer, by "the contradictory themes of social inequality and injustice, unbridled aggression, compassion, playfulness and hope."

Shakur's career took off in 1991 with the November release of his first album, *2Pacalypse Now*. By the time he dropped his third LP, *Me Against the World*, in March, 1995, he was the standard bearer for gangsta rap and hip hop.

An adage says if you live by the sword, you die by the sword. Others, like myself, believe: You can take the boy out of New York City but you can't take New York City out of the boy. Tupac put it best: Only God can judge me.

On the night of September 7, 1996, Shakur attended a Mike Tyson boxing match in Las Vegas. Driving to a club after the fight, a white Cadillac pulled alongside his vehicle and Shakur was shot four times, with one bullet piercing his lung. As he lie gravely wounded, the police arrived. Tupac, true to his code to the end, looked up at the cops and said, "Fuck you."

They turned out to be his last words.

SET ONE

December 31, 1990

Of the Grateful Dead, sax great Branford Marsalis once observed: "Guys who play jazz and don't only listen to jazz know those guys."

The Dead's last great New Year's Eve show — among countless fantastic New Year's Eve shows — took place on December 31, 1990 at the Oakland Coliseum. Since the Dead only played one more New Year's Eve gig (the following year), that's not really going out on a limb, is it ?

The night was stolen by Marsalis. The Branford Marsalis Quartet opened the show and were joined by Bruce Hornsby for their set. Branford would later sit in with the Dead for their second set, which included an after-midnight rave through "Not Fade Away", "Eyes of the World", "Dark Star."

Branford is as nice as he is funny, which is why he got on so well with Jerry. He did a hilarious imitation of Garcia; he had the joy-infused pitch of Jerry's voice down pat. Using that voice, Branford described how, backstage on the night of the historic March 29, 1990 show at Nassau (hands down, one of the greatest Dead shows *ever*), the guitarist attempted to teach him "Bird Song" moments before walking onstage: "Okay, man, we're gonna play it like this ... *dit, dit, dit* ... and in this key ... *dat, dat, dat*."

Branford loved to tell the story of Deadheads anonymously calling him at home about the March 29 gig: "I got people calling my house — 'That was a fantastic show.'

"'Hey, how did you get this number?'

"'We're everywhere, man. But don't worry about it. We're harmless.'"

Of the March 29 gig, Marsalis recalls, "Jerry and I hit it off [onstage]. He noticed that a lot of things I was playing were based on things I heard him playing. He was grinning."

Late 1991

After the deaths of artist Rick Griffin and Bill Graham in separate accidents in late 1991, Jerry paid a visit to Best Comics, a high-end comix, comic book and concert poster store on Haight Street, not far from Ashbury Street. Jerry was an avid comix and comic book collector who owned a complete set of EC Comics and was a regular at the store. The owner and Jerry were old friends, and both were close with Griffin.

Walking hand-in-hand with the light the Grateful Dead cast was a darkness. It hovered over, and around, the band, manifesting itself in loss and sorrow — Altamont, Lenny Hart, the untimely passing of band members, the tragic deaths of Adam Katz, Griffin and Graham.

John Barlow put it this way: "The other side will have its way. If you're going to manifest a lot of light, someone's got to pay the bill."

On that brisk autumn day in late 1991. the shop owner recalls, "Jerry told me he was losing his sense of direction."

A little more than six months later, following the Grateful Dead's summer tour in 1992, Garcia again became deathly ill, for a time slipping in and out of consciousness at his home. After having cardiac tests done, he was told he had an enlarged heart. Jerry slowly regained his health at his home with the aid of a support team; he stopped using heroin, cut down on smoking, adopted a vegan diet, and dropped 70 pounds.

After a 16-year run, Best Comics closed in 1992, one less haven for Jerry to retreat to. The losses of Griffin, Graham and Brent, his own health woes, and the closing of his favorite comics hang-out all within an 18-month period left the guitarist shaken.

Made acutely aware of mortality, Garcia regained his "sense of direction" in the last three years of his life by prioritizing the pursuits that made him happy. He drew and painted (on canvas and the computer), pursued scuba diving and swimming, and traveled to Ireland. Jerry still harboured dreams of bringing *The Sirens of Titan* to the screen, remarking, "I have all the patience in the world about *Sirens*. For me, it's not a Grateful Dead project, it's a 'Me project.'"

He wrote his childhood memoir, *Harrington Street*, as well as several formidable new songs with Hunter (among them, "Days Between" and "So Many Roads"), attempted to start an improvisational band with Edie Brickell and Bruce Hornsby, and made it clear to those around him he wanted to leave the Grateful Dead.

Garcia investigated the earliest applications of virtual reality, immersed himself in permaculture (sustainable living), and made peace with most of the women in his life with whom he had had a substantive relationship: Sara Ruppenthal (his first wife), Barbara Meier, who Jerry met through Robert Hunter and dated in the early 1960s, and Deborah Koons, a filmmaker and producer he first met in 1975 when they were working on *The Grateful Dead Movie*.

Autumn, 1992

That Garcia is being held hostage by the Grateful Dead has been obvious for years. Jerry isn't blind. He can see that the Dead are stultifying. But any murmur of taking a break — as they did in 1974 (following an October 20, 1974 show, the band began a self-imposed exile from performing; over the next 22 months, they played just four concerts) — to rethink and revitalize the Dead is met by laying a huge guilt trip on Jerry.

They bring out the babies, the kids, the hospital bills. "We've all got families !" Big wringing of the hands and weeping. There's a huge jones there for the money. Everyone who works for the Dead has been so well paid for so long they can't let [Garcia], the cash cow, go to pasture.

They have mortgages and car payments and all this has swamped the original ideals of the band.

In the old days, adventure and infinite possibility were [their] missions. For a long time, anarchic mischief propelled [them]. It was a magic force. But [then] the Dead became engulfed and paralyzed by the forces of chaos they once rode. It seemed as the years went by, it got harder to do anything other than go the same old places.

SET ONE

It seems that everything that starts out as genuine in America eventually ... starts selling tickets to itself.

Authenticity is just about the most marketable thing going. And, by God, Jerry had it.

The Grateful Dead [have] always been and always will be Jerry Garcia.

— *Playboy*, in memorandum

December, 1995

In the late 1980s, Dr. Randy Baker was retained by Jerry at his own expense to travel with him when the Grateful Dead were on the road. Baker was experienced in every aspect of health care and meticulously educated, having earned a biology degree from Stanford University and a Medical Doctorate from the University of Michigan's School of Medicine, where he served his residency in Family Practice. He was certified by the American Board of Holistic Medicine and had also completed four years of post-graduate education at the Hahnemann College of Homeopathy.

Garcia had asked the Dead organization to pay for Baker's traveling expenses so he could accompany him on tour, but Baker was viewed by many in the Dead's "camp," including band members, as a scam artist of sorts, a thirty-something Deadhead pulling off the ultimate Deadhead ruse — free tickets, all access passes, and a daily audience with Jerry. The idea was shot down by the Dead organization, forcing Garcia to foot the bill for Baker's expenses. "[Our] proposal was turned down," Baker would later tell Robert Greenfield. "I wasn't given any reasons."

The onset of coronary arterial disease and diabetes, the long-term effects of his heroin use, and his attempt to cold turkey himself off the opiate following the summer, 1992 tour all combined to nearly kill Garcia following the tour. Both the guitarist and Baker agreed that Garcia was nowhere near fit enough to go on the road for the fall, 1992 tour. His body was just beginning to heal as a result of proper rest, nutrition and exercise.

After Jerry let the band know that he was thinking of canning the tour, members of the band and organization responded with another mantra Garcia had grown tired of hearing: Too many people will be hurt financially if we cancel.

The roadies, the sound crew, the GDTS and GDM staffs, Dennis McNally, the managers, the accountants, the lawyers ... approximately 50 dependents in all.

Late in the summer of 1992, Phil and his wife, Jill, arranged for a female doctor to go Garcia's home to evaluate his health. Lesh and other members of the band had been pressuring Garcia to replace Baker with this doctor, who, after a brief physical, declared that, with two more weeks of rest, Jerry would be physically fit and able to tackle the fall tour.

Less than two hours after the doctor's arrival, Garcia asked her to leave. He had reached his wit's end with the pressure to replace Baker with a person he saw as a charlatan, someone who could be easily manipulated and had anything but his best interests at heart.

Twenty-five years later, in the Amir Bar-Lev documentary, *Long Strange Trip* (2017), Lesh would candidly, and contritely, admit: "What we should have done was take a break."

Angered by the power play, Jerry finally sided with Baker and decided to cancel the tour. Garcia instructed Manasha Matheson to call the Dead's office and inform them of his decision. The move riled more than several people in the camp, who searched for someone to scapegoat.

Like Randy Baker, Manasha was looked down upon — ostracized would be more like it — by most insiders; she would later be disparaged in books by both Dennis McNally (who Jerry privately abhorred) and Steve Parish. In his 2004 memoir, Parish admitted members of the "Dead family" actively conspired to get rid of Matheson. (For the record, Parish would, years later, apologize to her.)

Jerry may have groused to a friend or two with an ear about the difficulties of his relationship, but who doesn't complain about their relationship occasionally ? For the record, he loved Matheson, a fact lost on many around them. In the summer of 1990, he drove her to the top of Mt. Talmapais at sunset and asked her to marry him (she refused, telling him she preferred to "marry free of legal convention;" the couple were married in a civil ceremony in the garden of their San Anselmo home on August 17, 1990).

When the Grateful Dead prematurely returned to the road in early December, 1992, starting with a series of shows in Denver, McNally, knowing Matheson would be in Marin attending to the 5-year-old child she had with Garcia in 1987, used an organization account to pay the airfare for poet Barbara Meier to fly to the gigs and meet Garcia. Meier had already made inroads back into Jerry's life: she had been a backstage guest since 1991 and had recently interviewed him for *Tricycle* magazine. In Denver, according to Greenfield, she issued an ultimatum to Jerry: "*Are we going to do this or what ?*"

The typically non-confrontational Garcia responded, "Let's go for it."

McNally's ploy had worked. Before December was over, Garcia left Matheson for Meier. One observer later described the internally-orchestrated chain of events as a "flat-out coup."

In April, 1993, Garcia parted ways with Meier for Deborah Koons. Meier had been a major influence on Jerry's life during his formative years as a musician. According to Ms. Meier, "[Jerry] said, 'What do you need ?' I gave him an amount, and he said, 'How 'bout double that ?' I never saw him again."

Matheson and the team of care-providers she had assembled around Jerry — Baker, Gloria DiBiase, Vince DiBiase, Lyn Heineken and Brian Quigley — had provided stability for Garcia. They were people who unconditionally loved and cared for him, bathing and grooming him as he recovered. Without Matheson and her crew around, Garcia was unmoored. When the Dead returned to the road in the spring of 1993, he began to smoke cigarettes and use heroin again.

Koons, who Jerry had resumed a relationship with in the spring of 1993 and married in early 1994, saw Garcia as a business opportunity. She was interested in tying his vast fortune to her wealth to start a production company, which, fortunately, never came to pass. To her credit, Koons confronted him about his heroin use at least once, and he abruptly left her for a brief period.

Garcia spent the last two years of his life pleading with the band in organizational meetings to release him from his contract and allow him to exit the Grateful Dead. Joe McCord confirms this: "One of the things that is very important for people to know is that Jerry wanted to quit the Dead."

According to McCord, two Grateful Dead employees corroborate his allegation, each stating they possess copies of the minutes from the organizational meetings during which Garcia asked to be let go.

The band refused.

He was crushed. His body and soul began to whittle away. "He was just shriveling in front of our eyes," recalls former Bill Graham Presents vice president Bob Barsotti. "You could see it."

Just before the summer, 1995 tour, Garcia, at long last, recognized the need for acute change and agreed to Baker's proposal of entering an inpatient treatment facility after the tour. He kept his word, heading to the Betty Ford Clinic (which had been recommended by Koons) in mid-July. But after two weeks, he asked Koons and Baker if he could check out early to celebrate his 53rd birthday at home.

Although he had been weaned off heroin, which is why Baker and Koons agreed to his request, his body was in desperate shape. And Jerry knew it. He had been complaining, with good reason, that the Ford Clinic lacked the medical facilities needed to address his most pressing condition — his failing body.

Home again, he told Koons, "My body's shot."

In the Bar-Lev film, Trixie Garcia summarized it best, and from the perspective of a daughter who lost her father to the machinery of the Grateful Dead industrial complex, when she stated: "I just wish he could have gotten some fucking rest."

1993

Stephen Cripe is one of the more interesting, important, but lesser-known folks in Grateful Dead legend.

Cripe, who hailed from Pasco County in the Tampa Bay area of Florida, was a woodworker, Deadhead and self-taught luthier. Between 1991 and 1993, he built a guitar based on sketches he made of Tiger by freeze-framing the Grateful Dead video, *So Far*, so he could forge an image.

According to dozin.com, Cripe built an "instrument [that] honored Garcia's interest in preserving rain forests, using recycled rosewood originally harvested in Brazil for the fingerboard. For the guitar's body, Cripe said he reused East Indian rosewood ... unlike most guitars, this one's neck consisted of one solid piece of rosewood extending all the way through the center of the body."

In 1993, with the aid of a common friend, Cripe sent the guitar — which would come to be known as Lightning Bolt, as it featured an inlay of the 13-point lightning bolt — to David Grisman, who forwarded it to Jerry. The guitarist's representatives contacted the Floridian, telling him that Garcia was "intrigued" by the guitar. The truth was, Jerry was so "intrigued" that he had already begun playing it onstage with the Grateful Dead !

"Garcia was amazed when it came around at the guesswork [Cripe] had to make — and got right — to give that guitar Irwin's look and feel," Bobby told *Guitar Aficionado*. "It was astounding."

Jerry handed the six-string over to San Francisco guitar technician Gary Brawer so he could replace the electronics. Upon receiving it back from Brawer, Garcia declared, "[This is] the guitar I've always been waiting for."

Cripe was asked by Jerry to build another guitar, but he had forgotten to photograph Lightning Bolt. In a panic, he called Garcia, who told him, "Just do it. If I don't like it, I'll send it back."

Again, with little knowledge of Jerry's guitar specs, he built a second guitar, which came to be known as Top Hat. Garcia loved it, sending him a check for $6,500. The brilliant Steve Kimock also became a fan, and still plays Cripe guitars.

Tragically, Mr. Cripe was killed at age 42 in a May, 1996 fireworks accident in Florida, which is both sad and ironic, as all his guitars had an exploding firecracker on the head. Adding to the irony: Tampa Bay derives its name from the Native American term for "Sticks of Fire," as it is known for lightning storms. Its NHL team is named the Lightning.

The Florida luthier was invited to meet Jerry backstage at a Dead show in Miami in 1994. They discussed Top Hat. Cripe recalls, "He said, 'It was almost like I sent you the specs for what I was really looking for in a guitar.'"

September 20, 1993

Jerry, energized and enchanted by singer Edie Brickell's guest appearance with the Grateful Dead on the night of September 20, 1993, launched into a dramatic "Morning Dew" as his muse exited the Madison Square Garden stage.

In 1993, Garcia had become invigorated by the idea of starting a new band that would feature live improvisation from a group of supremely-gifted musicians. Adding to his vigor: for the first time in almost a decade, his health was no longer an issue.

Jerry was drawn to a number of remarkable musicians who had either guested with the Grateful Dead or recorded with him. He put into action a plan to assemble a band of cracker-jack cats who could make up music on the fly — among them, Bruce Hornsby, Branford Marsalis, bassist Rob Wasserman and the vocalist Brickell, formerly of the New Bohemians.

"I [have] this idea of putting together a band that [doesn't] have any material, nothing worked out — just the extreme version," Garcia told Anthony DeCurtis of *Rolling Stone*. "Edie's actually prepared to do this. She's even ready to have people in the audience say, 'I want you to use these words,' or, 'I want you to make this the subject of the song.'"

Garcia and Ms. Brickell had recorded the songs "Zillionaire" and "American Popsicle" for Wasserman's 1994 solo album, *Trios*, which featured the long-time RatDog bass player recording as part of various musical threesomes. (Hornsby and Marsalis also joined Wasserman, laying down a version of Bruce's "White Wheeled Limousine," as did Bobby and Neil Young for the Weir-Willie Dixon blues, "Eternity").

"American Popsicle" featured Jerry and Brickell improvising with Wasserman; the song might best be described as Garcia playing the uncharted guitar figures that populated the "space" segments of Grateful Dead concerts with Ms. Brickell singing what could be described as Native American chants and wails along with jazzy vocal scats. Mr. Wasserman superbly, and subtly, plays counterpoint to Jerry's electrifying runs.

Brickell and Garcia connected on both a musical and personal level. He invited her to sing with the Grateful Dead on September 20; that night, before a congregation of 20,000, she joined Jerry and Phil during "space," quietly offering several gentle vocal improvs. After Weir and Vince joined in, Brickell's excursions became more sinuous, snaking in and out of the musical discordance.

As Garcia played the riff to "The Other One," Brickell remained onstage, making up lyrics about "sneaking out the back stairs" and wanting to "see what's going on on the top floor." She remained silent during the remainder of "The Other One" before adding some beautiful background vocals on "Going Down the Road Feeling Bad."

Like most things in the last few years of his life, if there was a novel idea Garcia wanted to explore, the answer from those around him was an emphatic "No." Take a respite from touring ? *No way*, decreed the crowd. Start a new group with Edie Brickell ? *Not a chance*, ruled the temperamental Koons, a cunning, and controlling, business woman and person. She put a resounding and immediate kibosh on the supergroup idea, and it, sadly, fell by the wayside.

For Garcia, tired of being told by others what he could and could not do with his life, it was another small but devastating blow.

1994

It's no secret that Jerry loved reading fiction, with a fondness for science fiction.

"My Pretty Pony" is a 1989 short story written by fiction novelist Stephen King that centers on a dying man's attempt to convey the essence of life to his grandson by comparing the beauty, and linear nature, of life to a pretty pony. The short was later included in a 1993 collection of King's work, *Nightmares and Dreamscapes*.

In 1994, Jerry was among a group of "celebrities," including Matthew Broderick, Tim Curry and Kathy Bates, who read and recorded stories from *Nightmares and Dreamscapes*.

Jerry recited "My Pretty Pony" using varying voice inflections to convey the twists and turns of the story's plot and succinct message: Time, and life, are fleeting.

Garcia was very unhappy, and equally unhealthy, in 1994 and 1995, continuing to use heroin and smoke cigarettes. He also repeatedly expressed his desire to leave the Grateful Dead to his bandmates and GDP, which was always denied. As best as I can discern, Jerry and the other four core members of the Grateful Dead had signed individual, binding, and multiple-year contracts with GDP that, likely, extended beyond 1995, with each drawing an equal salary based on concert ticket revenue, merchandising, record company income, and so on. (Song-writing royalties are paid out individually.)

It's my belief Jerry knew he was dying (which is why he reached for Tiger to play the "Box of Rain" encore In Chicago on July 9, 1995). Robert Hunter has stated the same, citing as "proof" a phone call he received from Garcia shortly before he passed away; during the conversation, Jerry paid the lyricist the ultimate compliment: "Your words never stuck in my throat."

No different than the call to Hunter, Garcia's 53-minute reading of "My Pretty Pony" is his way of saying farewell to us. Jerry loved Deadheads and wished he could've been more accessible to us.

Like the old man speaking with his grandchild, Garcia's "parting message" is clear: Value life, love life and each other, and live life.

Summer, 1994

Jerry had a lot of respect for pantomime Joe McCord, whose friendship he valued, seeing to it that Joe was a regular visitor to his digs. The guitarist knew the discourse would be lively, the laughs abundant, and the opinions honest. He never once discussed, or used, heroin around Joe. In fact, it was only after Jerry died that McCord learned his friend had been using the opiate. Instead, Garcia would talk about "needing my guitar." Like scuba diving, hanging out or jamming with Bobby, or shooting the breeze with Joe, playing the guitar in private was one of the few ways for Garcia to get to that place where he could be free of the world and its smothering demands.

Joe last saw Jerry in the summer of 1994. "I had a visit with [him] a little over a year from his death. He was very unhappy. He told me that he wanted to retire from the band, paint, draw, write his memoirs, and play with his friends in his living room. He told me that he wanted to quit, but the band had him over a contractual barrel and wouldn't let him quit. He said very cryptically, 'The only way to quit the Dead is to be dead.'"

Joe re-affirmed this in a 2015 interview with the website janglinsouls.com: "He wanted to quit playing music professionally. But the Grateful Dead, the rest of the band, wouldn't let him go. I guess his words came true. It was horrible … an ugly ending to their relationship."

He shakes his head.

"It was a Greek Tragedy."

July 16, 1995

Bob Dylan was ecstatic to see Jerry backstage at the Grateful Dead's concert in Highgate, Vermont on June 15, 1995. (The folk-rock pioneer was there to serve as the Dead's opening act.) A pair of recently unearthed black-and-white photos from photographer Mark Haworth Harlan capture the moment perfectly as the two exchange handshakes, big smiles and mighty hugs.

At Highgate, Garcia and Dylan excitedly discussed a new project: a Jimmie Rodgers tribute album that the Minnesota native was putting together. Weeks earlier, in a hand-written letter from Dylan to Jerry, he had asked Garcia to contribute a song to the album.

Rodgers, an idol to both Dylan and Jerry, is known as "The Father of Country Music." He was wildly popular in America during the early 20th century and long after his death in May, 1933 from tuberculosis. Born in Meridian, Mississippi in 1897, Rodgers was known for his rhythmic yodeling style.

Here is Dylan's letter:

My record company (a very limited one) is doing a Jimmie Rodgers tribute record — you don't have to yodel — there's plenty of songs where he doesn't yodel but if you want to yodel, that's ok too — Anyway one of the performers on this record will be me and of course the perfect song for me is Blue Eyed Jane. And it's included with this letter — Did ya hear my version of "Two Soldiers" ? Anyway if it's not too much to ask, think about a Jimmie song — let me know something in some kind of incalculated amount of time — whatever you decide is ok with me —

All the best —

Bob --

SET ONE

On July 16, 1995, Jerry, David Grisman and John Kahn entered Grisman's studio and recorded "Blue Yodel #9 (Standing on the Corner)" for the Dylan-curated album, *The Songs of Jimmie Rodgers — A Tribute*.

The July 16 recording of the song is historically significant in both the Grateful Dead and the music worlds for two reasons. First, the session is the last known recording by Garcia, who rushed to complete the track before entering the Ford Clinic.

Of the session, Grisman would write in *Dupree's Diamond News* that Jerry was in a playful mood, imploring him: "'Talk to me, David … you should talk to me a little bit in my solo …'

"Garcia was asking me to converse with him musically during the guitar solo he'd been playing after the first verse of 'Blue Yodel #9,' [which] we had never played together before.

"'Hi, Jerry, nice solo you're playing,' I quipped. We were kidding around, exchanging light-hearted banter like we always did when we got together in the small recording room that used to be my garage."

Garcia's voice is bubbly and exuberant. conveying the joy he feels at singing the Rodgers gem, but cracks when he attempts to hit the yodeling part of the refrain.

The second reason the session is historically significant: While it is widely accepted that the last guitar Jerry played onstage with the Grateful Dead was Tiger, the last guitar Garcia played in the studio was a vintage blonde archtop acoustic 1939 Gibson Super 400 N.

According to archtop.com, the archtop acoustic Gibson Super 400 model used by Garcia was available "in natural finish [and] by special order as far back as 1936, but only a handful were produced, and the blonde finish option wasn't offered in the catalog until 1939. Along with the new finish, Gibson announced the redesign of the Super 400, abandoning the vibrant X-braced soundboard of the prewar models. Only a scant few of the blonde guitars were produced before the company redesigned the model for parallel bracing."

Jerry would pass away a little more than three weeks after using the Gibson Super 400 N to lay down "Blue Yodel #9."

Dylan had made it clear in his hand-written note to Garcia that he was going to record "Blue Eyed Jane" for the LP and, by all accounts, was thrilled when Jerry contributed "Blue Yodel #9" (one of Rodgers' most popular tunes), selected by the Rock and Roll Hall of Fame + Museum as one of the 500 songs that shaped rock-n-roll.

By asking Garcia to record a song for the Rodgers album, Dylan was, once again, demonstrating his immense respect for Jerry, whom, I believe, he considered a rare equal.

June 21, 1995

On the first day of summer, 1995, the Grateful Dead performed their last great show.

They played only 14 songs.

At the Knickerbocker Arena in Albany, the band got their game on early with a charged "Hell in a Bucket" opener from Weir, looking buff in a black muscle shirt and grey shorts. There's a two-minute break before Jerry drops the opening notes to the sinister "Loser."

His vocals are clear and strong, with each note pronounced. Garcia's hair is shoulder-length and beautifully styled, his beard thick and full, both one hundred percent white. His new eyeglasses complement his face, and his brown trousers were a step up from the sweatpants he had been wearing.

In Greek mythology, Atlas was a Titan condemned by Zeus to hold up the sky for eternity as punishment for warring against the Olympians. When the burden became too great, Atlas asked the Greek hero Perseus (the son of Zeus) to help him put an end to his struggle.

Perseus had beheaded Medusa and was transporting her head inside a knapsack to Polydectes. Atlas asked to be shown the head, knowing that by looking into her eyes, he would turn to stone.

Like Atlas, Garcia has been carrying a burden — the incessant touring and demands on his life — he can no longer bear. At the Albany show, Jerry is diminutive in stature. Like a pencil that has been sharpened to a nub, he's a shell of his former-self.

It's a fair question to ask: Wasn't it obvious to the Grateful Dead, the band's organization, and his wife, Deborah Koons, that Garcia was in a severely-compromised state of health and was, literally, dying right in front of their eyes ? He was just seven weeks from death. Jerry may have been his own worst enemy, but he deserved a far better fate than the one cast for him by those around him.

Weir knocks it out of the park on "Take Me to the River," co-written by Al Green and Mabon "Teenie" Hodges in 1974 and popularized by the Talking Heads four years later. Garcia's solos are fluid and perky; at one point, he even shows a little flash, running his left hand up and down the fretboard ala Eddie Van Halen. Behind him, Mickey, in an orange T-shirt, is thumping away. After the song, Jerry stands isolated from the band, his back to the audience, fiddling with his amp. Unless he was smoking a cigarette, this was not typical on-stage behavior for Garcia.

The turning point of the concert comes next, with a beautiful, but melancholy, 15-minute rendition of "Row, Jimmy." It's here Garcia begins to wield his power. It's been his band since Pigpen's death and tonight he has decided to remind everyone of that. He looks to his right, one of the few times he gazes at the band, but at no one in particular. Garcia controls the tempo and timing of the song, drawing it out where he pleases, emphasizing certain vocal and instrumental passages as he sees fit. He is deliberate and the song as delicate as a spring sheet of ice on a New England pond.

Not only does Jerry minimally interact with the band, he hardly looks up from his guitar. He plays hunched over, as if inspecting each note, his neck craned, chin pinned to his chest and hair hanging down. On "Row, Jimmy," he uses the MIDI on his first solo, eliciting a flute sound. During the second instrumental passage, he freestyles on guitar, independent of the band, as if playing by and for himself. The result is a wonderful but blue four-and-a-half-minute solo, tenderly developed and nurtured by Garcia. Vince Welnick, on electric piano, does a gorgeous two-step with Jerry, who ends his solo by stepping to the mic to gingerly sing: "Broken heart, don't feel so bad …"

The audience, recognizing the poignancy of Jerry's extended soloing and the emotional resonance in his voice, responds with cascades of applause.

Phil, tall and thin, his hair dyed a brownish blonde, looks fantastic. He interrupts the Weir-Garcia trade-off with "Broken Arrow." Intuition was one of the qualities that made the Grateful Dead great and Lesh knows Garcia has set out on his own tonight. Phil complements the emotional tenor of the evening with a sublime take on the Robbie Robertson song.

To his credit, Vince shines here, and throughout the night, on the electric piano. Unfortunately, time seems to have harshly judged Mr. Welnick's tenure in the Dead. With Hornsby in the band for Vince's first year-and-a-half, he performed without drawing too much attention to himself or his playing. Without Bruce around, Vince was more exposed. In his defense, Welnick was hamstrung by not being able to use the Hammond B-3 onstage. (As was the case with Keith Godchaux, who, after replacing his acoustic piano with an electric one, learned there are only so many textures and sounds an electric piano can produce.) And, like Keith, who had the misfortune to follow Pigpen, Vince had the equally-difficult task of following Brent.

A tight, powerhouse version of "The Promised Land" closes the set; Jerry rips it up on Chuck Berry's licks and Vince contributes a red-hot solo.

The second set begins with a jaw-dropping 28-minute "Scarlet Begonias", "Fire on the Mountain." The audience reaction to Jerry's soloing in "Scarlet Begonias" is loud and approving; buoyed, he stands more erect. At several points during the song, he's forced to look down to his left at the teleprompter to regain his place. During the bridge jam to "Fire on the Mountain," Garcia adds a little fuzz to his sound and then turns to the band, again without looking at anyone , to remind them: This is still my classroom, and I am still the teacher.

Garcia plays another lengthy solo in "Fire," dictating the timing and pace of the music, as he did earlier on "Row, Jimmy." He extends the jam, mostly with his chin pressed to his chest; at one point, he briefly stops playing and walks back to his amps to mess with something. Vince fills the empty space with a pretty solo. As with "Row, Jimmy," there is a transformational moment here, which lasts almost a minute: It occurs when Jerry stops playing altogether and just sings the chorus, adding several plaintive, sorrow-filled wails.

Late in the second set, he looks over at the band one final time, once more making eye contact with no one, but this time he's saying: This has all been fun, but now it's time for me to say goodbye. He strums the opening chords to the Grateful Dead's final performance of "Morning Dew."

Garcia is as powerful as he can be in his compromised state of health, summoning all his strength, and greatness, for one final, and riveting, "Dew." Like Babe Ruth at the end of his career, he is broken down and beat up. Jerry and the Babe, two great American immortals crushed by the albatross of fame, both giving their all until there was no more to give. On May 25, 1935, in the second-to-last game of Ruth's Hall of Fame career, the Sultan of Swat, as a Boston Brave, went 4-for-4 and blasted three home runs.

Tonight is Garcia's three-homer farewell game.

July 9, 1995

The last known photo of Jerry was snapped just moments after he exited the stage at Soldier Field on July 9, 1995. He's striding along in a black jacket and black shorts, cigarette in his left hand, tugging at his beard with his right hand.

Jerry is following a well-armed plain-clothes Chicago police officer in a blue-and-white windbreaker sporting a .45 in a side holster, a badge on his left hip, a taser in a rear pocket. Garcia is making tracks toward the Grateful Dead's limousines.

As the Jimi Hendrix version of "The Star-Spangled Banner" plays over the stadium PA, a firework display lights up the Chicago night. The other members of the Dead find their way to Jerry.

For the five core members, looking at the colorful explosions in the sky, it's their last moment together, having spent the past 30 years creating something both beautiful and enduring.

"The last time I saw Jerry, we were hugging after the [July 9] show and he slapped me on the back and said, 'Always a hoot, always a hoot,'" Weir told film documentarian Mike Fleiss. "Those were his last words to me."

August 9, 1995

The night Garcia passed away, Bobby had a premonition. In a dream, he had happened upon "invisible paint" and was attempting to share the discovery with his friend: "'Hey, Jerry, look — invisible paint. [But] he was intent on something, he was searching for something."

Mr. Weir, more so than any other member of the Grateful Dead, was connected to Garcia both on and off the stage. "Jerry was basically my older brother," Bob told Mike Fleiss. "What we had was thicker than blood. We didn't need to talk to know how each other was feeling."

Early on, Bobby recognized that Garcia had a highly-singular sound, style and gift. He elected to seek out unique ways to support Jerry's on-stage genius, enabling him, with unparalleled modestly, to provide the sounds, colors, palettes, odd chord structures and off-beat time signatures to augment the guitarist's wizardry. "I was listening to Bill Evans [and] McCoy Tyner and I listened to the way they chorded, especially McCoy Tyner, the way he played under John Coltrane," Bob explained to Fleiss. "I was there to play chords and rhythms for Jerry to play over the top of."

Twenty-plus years later, Bob still struggles with the loss of his close pal. "Life has endless depth to it," he notes, "and making sense of all of that is something I'm taking my time doing."

Robert Hunter once observed: "In retrospect, I think Weir was hardest hit of the old crowd by [Jerry's] death ... Bob took it right on the chin. Shock was written all over his face for a long time, for any with eyes to see."

Offstage, Bobby's role in Garcia's life was much less complex. "As his friend, I just tried to keep him happy."

August 9, 1995 II

Wild is a 2014 Academy Award-nominated film directed by Jean-Marc Vallee that stars Oscar-winner Reese Witherspoon and the sensational Laura Dern. The plot follows a young woman as she hikes the Pacific Crest Trail and features a moving sequence that unfolds on August 9, 1995 — the day Jerry died.

The movie is based on author Cheryl Strayed's memoir, *Wild: Lost and Found on the Pacific Crest Trail* (2012), a *New York Times* best seller. In the film, the Witherspoon character —Strayed — is devastated by her recent divorce and the loss of her mom. She decides to hike 1,100 miles of the 2,650-mile trail through the heat of the Mojave and snow of Mt. Hood on a journey of self-discovery.

After 94 days, Strayed, who legally changed her last name because of her marital infidelities and reckless lifestyle, emerges from the trail in the small Oregon town of Ashland. There, she spies a group of Deadheads sitting around a guitarist who's playing an acoustic and singing "Box of Rain."

As the crowd grows around him, Strayed walks over to a newspaper stand to discover headlines announcing Garcia's passing.

A young man approaches and asks if she would like to attend a memorial for Jerry being held later that evening in a small club. She agrees and as she enters the club, a duo— Dusted and Eric D. Johnson (Fruit Bats) — are onstage playing electric guitar and singing a slightly re-worked version of "Ripple" that the pair certainly do justice to.

Film director Vallee beautifully incorporates music throughout *Wild*, principally the Simon and Garfunkel cover, "El Condor Pasa (If I Could)," while also employing the most effective use of Grateful Dead music in a movie since "Ripple" was featured in *Mask*, the 1985 Peter Bogdanovich film starring Cher, Eric Stoltz and the afore-mentioned, and always delightful, Ms. Dern.

Strayed's coming-of-age saga on the Pacific Crest Trail parallels the experiences of countless Deadheads who've set out on the Great American Highway to follow the music and figure their own shit out.

September 21, 1995

"There's no way to measure his greatness or magnitude as a person or as a player. I don't think eulogizing will do him justice. He was that great – much more than a superb musician with an uncanny ear and dexterity. He is the very spirit personified of whatever is muddy river country at its core and screams up into the spheres. He really had no equal.

"To me he wasn't only a musician and friend, he was more like a big brother who taught and showed me more than he'll ever know. There are a lot of spaces and advances between the Carter family, Buddy Holly and, say, Ornette Coleman, a lot of universes, but he filled them all without being a member of any school. His playing was moody, awesome, sophisticated, hypnotic and subtle. There's no way to convey the loss. It just digs down really deep."

— Bob Dylan

set two

November 30 and December 1, 1967

Queens native Danny Fields famously signed and managed Iggy Pop and the Stooges, signed the MC5, and managed the Ramones.

Fields was a life-long and close friend of Linda McCartney, whom he memorialized in his 2000 book, *Linda McCartney: A Portrait*.

In the tome, Fields interviews Bobby about Linda's visit on November 30 and December 1, 1967 to 710 Ashbury Street, where she spent two days photographing the Grateful Dead.

"First of all, I remember her face. Just her face," Weir told Fields. "I remember her, yes. She pinned me right away, she wouldn't avert her gaze. I was the one who met her at the door at the Ashbury Street house when she came to photograph the band. Our manager had told us that Linda Eastman was coming by, that she was the Eastman Kodak heiress and a big-time photographer, a really good photographer.

"The word was that she was so pretty and so rich that someone was going to make a play for her eventually and take the prize. She took a lot of pictures of me that day, and then we were going to come back the next day, because some guys couldn't be there. But that night I was getting all kinds of heat from the band, they were convinced that she was the Linda Eastman of Eastman Kodak, and that since she took all these pictures of me she must have liked me, so the guys were pressuring me to hook up with her. 'Do it for your fellow band members,' they were saying. She was rich and we weren't; I suppose they wanted the band to marry into all this money. We were really broke.

"Their reasoning was, here was this attractive young single lady and we sort of had the same background, my family was well-to-do, so the guys thought it was a perfect match. They weren't kidding. I'd just left home the year before to go be a starving artist and I was pleased with what was happening, but the other guys had been starving for a little longer and it wasn't so much fun. They were actually trying to force-feed me to her, and it got a little uncomfortable for me and for her, you know how guys can be when they've got this plan.

"So, I just went up into the attic and hid. It was getting a little embarrassing, and I guess she was kind of feeling it, too. As if she were going to buy us equipment or something. The guys hammered each other all the time, and it was my turn. We couldn't afford a TV, so if we weren't on each other's cases we had nothing else to do. It was a way to keep ourselves amused.

"There was nothing romantic going on between me and Linda that day she was first there. I was nineteen, and maybe there was a little flirtation going on, but that's all. We talked about the quality of light - I'd never had a substantial conversation with a photographer before, and she was obviously way into it. I found it interesting to hear her talk about light and shadows and colours, and then we walked around the Panhandle [of Golden Gate Park] and just looked around. It was a whole new experience for me, to start looking at things through a visually oriented person's eyes.

"But there was definitely something that she had about her. She was maybe the only photographer that the guys could ever sit still for, for more than two or three minutes. When she was looking at you, it seemed as if she was staring into the window of your soul, she was looking around in there. I'm not sure about the other guys, but I certainly felt it. She was an old friend, even though we'd just met. There's probably less than half a dozen people like that in your whole lifetime. I'm a total believer in reincarnation, and I would be real surprised if Linda and I hadn't put in some time together in the past. There was that little flash of recognition. An old friend that you've just met, you know ?"

September, 1996

In 1995, Paul McCartney composed a short documentary film titled *Grateful Dead: A Photofilm*, made up of still shots of the band taken by his late wife, Linda McCartney (nee Eastman). The Beatle great had been in touch with Jerry about the work, but Garcia passed away before Paul could share the final product with him.

The photos were shot in late 1967 at 710 Ashbury Avenue, the Dead's communal home in the Haight-Ashbury, and during a May 5, 1968 concert in Central Park's fabled bandshell. According to Neil Strauss of *The New York Times*, the nine-minute film is "a moody, hypnotic piece."

Grateful Dead: A Photofilm had its American premiere at the New York Film Festival in September, 1996. In creating the short, according to Mr. Strauss, Paul was "initially spurred not by a love for the band, but by a love for his wife's photography."

McCartney never saw the Grateful Dead perform live but did venture to 710 Ashbury Avenue late one evening to say hello.

No one was home.

Before Sir Paul swept Linda off her feet, Phil went on a date with her in Manhattan in August, 1967. (Lesh would later joke: "At least she married another bass player.")

Using just four rolls of snapshots that Linda took of the Dead, McCartney put together *Grateful Dead: A Photofilm*. "If Andy Warhol can film the Empire State Building for three hours, I figure I can do something with four rolls of film," commented Paul.

The titles and credits are handwritten by McCartney, who uses music from *Anthem of the Sun* (with the vocals removed) in the film's background. The black-and-white photographs are, in Strauss' words, "juxtaposed, morphed into one another and put together like flip books so that band members seem to be moving. Other times, the camera slowly pans across faces in a magnified crowd photo, stopping at the most interesting character: a man in a trilby who looks like an undercover agent."

The idea came to Macca while looking through a series of Linda's photos that were focused on — who else ? — Bobby. "I noticed where she was trying to get a portrait of Bob Weir, she would take a whole roll of him, one photo after another," he told Strauss. "Of course, she only needed one shot, but in looking at the whole roll it looked like a movie. Your eyes almost ran it all together."

McCartney and Jerry were discussing the project when Garcia unexpectedly passed away in 1995. "I was just about to show the film to him," Paul said. "I'd been in correspondence with him, because he was a painter and I thought he'd like this. Unfortunately, I missed him. I suppose it [became] a little bit of a tribute to Jerry."

Summer, 1996

A year after Jerry's death, Robert Hunter penned this poignant letter to his songwriting partner; in his own words, Hunter was "writing a letter to a dead man, because it's hard to find a context to say things like this other than to imagine I have your ear, which, of course, I don't."

Dear JG,

It's been a year since you shuffled off the mortal coil and a lot has happened. It might surprise you to know you made every front page in the world. The press is still having fun, mostly over lawsuits challenging your somewhat ... umm ... patchwork Last Will and Testament. Annabelle didn't get the EC horror comic collection, which I think would piss you off as much as anything. Nor could Doug Irwin accept the legacy of the guitars he built for you because the tax-assessment on them, icon-enriched as they are, is more than he can afford short of selling them off. The upside of the craziness is: your image is selling briskly enough that your estate should manage something to keep various wolves from various familial doors, even after the lawyers are paid. How it's to be divided will probably fall in the hands of the judge. An expert on celebrity wills said in the news that yours was a blueprint on how not to make a will.

The band decided to call it quits. I think it's a move that had to be made. You weren't exactly a sideman. But nothing's for certain. Some need at least the pretense of retirement after all these years. Can they sustain it ?

We'll see.

I'm writing this from England, by the way. Much clarity of perspective to be had from stepping out of the scene for a couple of months. What isn't so clear is my own role, but it's really no more problematic than it has been for the last decade. As long as I get words on paper and can lead myself to believe it's not bullshit, I'm roughly content. I'm not exactly Mr. Business.

I decided to get a personal archive together to stick on that stagnating computer site we had. Really started pouring the mustard on. I'm writing, for crying out loud, my diary on it ! Besides running my ego full tilt (what's new ?), I'm trying to give folks some skinny on what's going down. I don't mean I'm busting the usual suspects left and right, but am giving a somewhat less than cautious overview and soapboxing more than a little. They appointed me webmaster, and I hope they don't regret it.

There are those in the entourage who quietly believe we're washed up without you. Even should time and circumstance prove it to be so, we need to believe otherwise long enough to get some self-sustaining operations going, or we'll never know for sure. It's [a] matter of self-respect. Maybe it's a long shot, but this whole fucking trip was a longshot from the start, so what else is new ?

Your funeral service was one hell of a scene. Maureen and I took Barbara [Meier] and Sara [Ruppenthal] in and sat with them. MG waited over at our place. Manasha and Keelin were also absent. None by choice. Everybody from the band said some words and Steve, especially, did you proud, speaking with great love and candor. Annabelle got up and said you were a genius, a great guy, a wonderful friend, and a shitty father — which shocked part of the contingent and amused the rest. After a while the minister said that that was enough talking, but I called out, from the back of the church, "Wait, I've got something !" and charged up the aisle and read this piece I wrote for you, my voice and hands shaking like a leaf. Man, it was weird looking over and seeing you dead !

A slew of books have come out about you and more to follow. Perspective is lacking. It's way too soon. You'd be amazed at the number of people with whom you've had a nodding acquaintance who are suddenly experts on your psychology and motivations. Your music still speaks louder than all the BS: who you were, not the messes you got yourself into. Only a very great star is afforded that much inspection and that much forgiveness.

There was so much confusion on who should be allowed to attend the scattering of your ashes that they sat around for four months. It was way too weird for this cowboy, who was neither invited nor desirous of going. I said good-bye with my poem at the funeral service. It was cathartic and I didn't need an anti-climax.

A surreal sidelight: Weir went to India and scattered a handful of your ashes in the Ganges as a token of your worldwide stature. He took a lot of flak from the fans for it, which must have hurt. A bunch of them decided to scapegoat him, presumably needing someplace to misdirect their anger over the loss of you. In retrospect, I think Weir was hardest hit of the old crowd by your death. I take these things in my stride, though I admit to a rough patch here and there.

Some of the guys have got bands together and are doing a tour. The fans complain it's not the same without you, and of course it isn't, but a reasonable number show up and have a pretty good time. The insane crush of the latter-day GD shows is gone and that's all for the best. From the show I saw, and reports on the rest, the crowd is discovering that the sense of community is still present, matured through mutual grief over losing you. This will evolve in more joyous directions over time, but no one's looking to fill your shoes.

SET TWO

No one has the presumption.

Been remembering some of the key talks we had in the old days, trying to suss what kind of a tiger we were riding, where it was going, and how to direct it, if possible. Driving to the city once, you admitted you didn't have a clue what to do beyond composing and playing the best you could. I agreed — put the weight on the music, stay out of politics, and everything else should follow. I trusted your musical sense and you were good enough to trust my words.

Trust was the whole enchilada, looking back.

Walking down Madrone Canyon in Larkspur in 1969, you said some pretty mind-blowing stuff, how we were creating a universe and I was responsible for the verbal half of it. I said maybe, but it was your way with music and a guitar that was pulling it off. You said "That's for now. This is your time in the shadow, but it won't always be that way. I'm not going to live a long time, it's not in the cards. Then it'll be your turn." I may be alive and kicking, but no pencil pusher is going to inherit the stratosphere that so gladly opened to you. Recalling your statement, though, often helped keep me oriented as my own star murked below the horizon while you streaked across the sky of our generation like a goddamned comet !

Though my will to achieve great things is moderated by seeing what comes of them, I've assigned myself the task of trying to honor the original vision. I'm not answerable to anybody but my conscience, which, if less than spotless, doesn't keep me awake at night. Maybe it's best, personally speaking, that the power to make contracts and deal the remains of what was built through the decades rests in other hands. I wave the flag and rock the boat from time to time, since I believe much depends on it, but will accept the outcome with equanimity.

Just thought it should be said that I no longer hold your years of self-inflicted decline against you. I did for a while, felt ripped off, but have come to understand that you were troubled and compromised by your position in the public eye far beyond anyone's powers to deal with. Star shit. Who can you really trust ? Is it you or your image they love ? No one can understand those dilemmas in depth except those who have no choice but to live them. You whistled up the whirlwind and it blew you away. Your substance of choice made you more malleable to forces you would have brushed off with a characteristic sneer in earlier days. Well, you know it to be so. Let those who pick your bones note that it was not always so.

… what you were is more startlingly apparent in your absence than ever it was in the last decade. I remember sitting in the waiting room of the hospital through the days of your first coma. Not being related, I wasn't allowed into the intensive care unit to see you until you came to and requested to see me. And there you were — more open and vulnerable than I'd ever seen you. You grasped my hand and began telling me your visions, the crazy densely packed phantasmagoria way beyond any acid trip, the demons and mechanical monsters that taunted and derided, telling you endless bad jokes and making horrible puns of everything — and then you asked, point blank, "Have I gone insane ?" I said "No, you've been very sick. You've been in a coma for days, right at death's door. They're only hallucinations, they'll go away. You survived."

"Thanks," you said. "I needed to hear that."

Your biographers aren't pleased that I don't talk to them, but how am I to say stuff like this to an interviewer with an agenda ? I sometimes report things that occur to me about you in my journal, as the moment releases it, in my own way, in my own time, and they can take what they want of that.

Obviously, faith in the underlying vision which spawned the Grateful Dead might be hard to muster for those who weren't part of the all-night rap sessions circa 1960-61 … sessions that picked up the next morning at Kepler's bookstore then headed over to the Stanford cellar or St. Mike's to continue over coffee and guitars. There were no hippies in those days and the beats had bellied up. There was only us vs. '50's consciousness. There [were] no jobs to be had if we wanted them. Just folk music and tremendous dreams. Yeah, we dreamed our way here. I trust it. So did you. Not so long ago we wrote a song about all that, and you sang it like a prayer.

"The Days Between."

Last song we ever wrote.

Context is lost, even now. The Sixties were a long time ago and getting longer. A cartoon version of our times satisfies public perception. Our continuity is misunderstood as some sort of strange persistence of an outmoded style. Beads, bell bottoms and peace signs. But no amount of pop cynicism can erase the suspicion, in the minds of the present generation, that something was going on once that was better than what's going on now. And I sense that they're digging for "what it is" and only need the proper catalyst to find it for themselves. Your guitar is like a compass needle pointing the strange way there. I'm wandering far afield from the intention of this letter, a year's report, but this year wasn't made up only of events following your death in some roughly chronological manner. It reached down to the roots of everything, shook the earth off, and inspected them. The only constant is the fact that you remain silent. Various dances are done around that fact.

Don't misconstrue me, I don't waste much time in grief. Insofar as you were able, you were an exponent of a dream in the continual act of being defined into a reality. You had a massive personality and talent to present it to the world. That dream is the crux of the matter, and somehow concerns beauty, consciousness and community. We were, and are, worthy insofar as we serve it. When that dream is dead, there'll be time enough for true and endless grief.

John Kahn died in May, same day Leary did. Linda called 911 and they came over and searched the house, found a tiny bit of coke and carted her off to jail in shock. If the devil himself isn't active in this world, there's sure something every bit as mean: institutional righteousness without an iota of fellow feeling. But, as I figure, that's the very reason the dream is so important — it's whatever is the diametric opposite of that.

Human kindness.

Trust me that I don't walk around saying "this was what Jerry would have wanted" to drive my points home. What you wanted is a secret known but to yourself. You said "yes" to what sounded like a good idea at the time, "no" to what sounded like a bad one. I see more of what leadership is about, in the absence of it. It's an instinct for good ideas. An aversion to bad ones. Compromise on indifferent ones. Power is another matter. Power is not leadership but coercion. People follow leaders because they want to.

I know you were often sick and tired of the conflicting demands made on you by contentious forces you invited into your life and couldn't as easily dismiss. You once said to me, in 1960, "just say yes to everybody and do what you damn well want." Maybe, but when every "yes" becomes an IOU payable in full, who's coffer is big enough to pay up ? "Fuck 'em if they can't take a joke !" would be a characteristic reply. Unfortunately, you're not around to explain what was a joke and what wasn't. It all boils down to signed pieces of paper with no punch lines appended.

I know what I'm saying in this letter can be taken a hundred ways. As always, I just say what occurs to me to say and can't say what doesn't. Could I write a book about you ? No. Didn't know you well enough. Let those who knew you even less write them. You were canny enough to keep your own self to yourself and let your fingers do the talking. Speaking of "personal matters" was never your shtick.

Our friendship was testy. I challenged you rather more than you liked, having a caustic tongue. In later years, you preferred the company of those capable of keeping it light and non-judgmental. I think it must always be that way with prominent and powerfully gifted persons. I don't say that, for the most part, your inner circle weren't good and true. They'd have laid down their lives for you. I'd have had to think about it. I mean, a star is a star is a star. There's no reality check. If the truth were known, you were too well loved for your own good, but that smacks of psychologizing and I drop the subject forthwith.

All our songs are acquiring new meanings. I don't deny writing with an eye to the future at times, but our mutual folk, blues and country background gave us a mutual liking for songs that dealt with sorrow and the dark issues of life. Neither of us gave a fuck for candy coated shit, psychedelic or otherwise. I never even thought of us as a "pop band." You had to say to me one day, after I'd handed over the *Eagle Mall* suite, "Look, Hunter — we're a goddamn dance band, for Christ's sake ! At least write something with a beat !" Okay. I handed over "Truckin'" next. How was I to know ? I thought we were silver and gold; something new on this Earth. But the next time I tried to slip you the heavy stuff, you actually went for it. Seems like you'd had the vision of the music about the same time I had the vision of the words, independently.

Terrapin.

Shame about the record, but the concert piece, the first night it was played, took me about as close as I ever expect to get to feeling certain we were doing what we were put here to do. One of my few regrets is that you never wanted to finish it, though you approved of the final version I eked out many years later. You said, apologetically, "I love it, but I'll never get the time to do it justice." I realized that was true. Time was the one thing you never had in the last decade and a half. Supporting the Grateful Dead plus your own trip took all there was of that. The rest was crashing time. Besides, as you once said, "I'd rather toss cards in a hat than compose." But man, when you finally got down on it, you sure knew how.

The pressure of making regular records was a creative spur for a long time, but poor sales put the economic weight on live concerts where new material wasn't really required, so my role in the group waned. A difficult time for me, being at my absolute peak and all. I had to go on the road myself to make a living. It was good for me. I developed a sense of self direction that didn't depend on the Dead at all. This served well for the songs we were still to write together. You sure weren't interested in flooding the market. You knew one decent song was worth a dozen cobbled together pieces of shit, saved only by arrangement. I guess we have a few of those too, but the percentage is respectably low. Pop songs come and go, blossom and wither, but we scored a piece of Americana, my friend. Sooner or later, they'll notice what we did doesn't die the way we do. I've always believed that and so did you. Once in a while we'd even call each other "Mister" and exchange congratulations. Other people are starting to record those songs now, and they stand on their own.

For some reason it seems worthwhile to maintain the Grateful Dead structures: Rex, the website, GDP, the Deadhead office, the studio ... even with the band out of commission. I don't know if this is some sort of denial that the game is finished, or if the intuitive impulse is a sound one. I feel it's better to have it than not, just in case, because once it's gone there's no bringing it back. The forces will disperse and settle elsewhere. A business that can't support itself is, of course, no business at all, just a locus of dissension, so the reality factor will rule. Diminished as we are without you, there is still some of the quick, bright spirit around. I mean, you wouldn't have thrown in your lot with a bunch of belly floppers, would you ?

Let me see — is there anything I've missed ? Plenty, but this seems like a pretty fat report. You've been gone a year now and the boat is still afloat. Can we make it another year ? What forms will it assume ?

It's all kind of exciting.

They say a thousand years are only a twinkle in God's eye.

Is that so ?

Missing you in a longtime way.

rh

— Robert Hunter

September 11, 2001

Someone once lambasted the Grateful Dead as mad scientists operating on the minds of America's youth with rusty scalpels. Paul Fiori was one of my younger friends, who I met through my youngest brother, Anthony, and Jeffrey Reich. The three were America's youth and I was the mad scientist with the rusty scalpel, performing brain salad surgery on their then-fragile, egg-shell minds.

Paul, who died in the World Trade Center on the morning of September 11, 2001, was more than a willing subject.

In the autumns of 1988 and 1989, when the Dead played those mega-residencies at Madison Square Garden, I was there every night and most nights it was with Paul. I enjoyed seeing the band with him because he could roll with the madness. I would park on 12th Avenue on the West Side of Manhattan, five blocks from the Garden, where Paul and I would step out of my car and into a street world populated by hookers, drug dealers and bad people. The surroundings never bothered me; I was Bronx-born and raised and a little seedy street action wasn't going to raise my eyebrows. Paul, who grew up in Valhalla, a quaint hamlet 25 miles north of the city, never noticed, either. It wasn't naïveté on his part; Paul was anything but naive. It was that he could bounce as well as anyone and no matter where I took him — the Garden, Yankee Stadium, Manhattan, Giants Stadium, road trips to see the Grateful Dead — his focus was on a good time, and I liked that best about him.

His parents. Lino and Mary, were a principal and a teacher, respectively. Paul would often lament, "My parents are too smart for me to get away with anything."

That didn't stop him from trying.

When his mom and dad would vacation in the summer, Paul would remain home so he could caddy at a slice of heaven known as Century Country Club in Purchase. While the Fioris were enjoying exotic world destinations, Paul would host an annual, and epic, summer party in his family's backyard that featured the Great Red Shark, regular performers at the Wetlands in the late 1980s. Two of the Shark's members (Cliff Mays and Jim Weingast) now perform in the Blues Roadhouse Orchestra, which regularly gigs at Garcia's inside the Capitol Theatre. (Jeffrey plays bass !) Paul, the Shark's biggest fan, would set up the band on the back porch, roll out a few kegs of beer, and orchestrate a good time that would last past midnight, or until the Valhalla police made their yearly entrance.

We tend to deify people in death, attributing qualities to the deceased and creating tales about them that are more fiction than fact. I don't need to do that with Paul. He was very real, and serious about life and his sprouting family, going about his business like Jerry playing the guitar: Straight up.

Paul and I had countless good times at Grateful Dead concerts. Two stories stand out. On July 10, 1989, we ventured to Giants Stadium to see the Dead. During the first set, the skies opened and a rainstorm, coupled with an amazing thunderstorm that featured several nearby land lightning strikes, ensued. In high school, Paul was an under-sized linebacker with more heart than talent who played with reckless abandon. Football instilled the macho-man mentality in him. But the Grateful Dead had a way of stripping away that tough-guy persona. At Giants Stadium, I was miserable and dripping wet but when I looked to my right, there was Paul, soaked and smiling, noodling in time to the music as rain cascaded off his shirtless body.

Another thing I liked about Paul was that he never needed to be babysat. When we would trip, drink or smoke, he would hold his liquor or stay grounded on acid. And, believe me, we got out there some nights, holding one after-show rap in the woods behind my backyard, drinking beer alongside a pond while praying for UFOs to arrive. At a Garden show in 1990, Paul and I were tripping when I noticed he had become fixated on something. We had loge seats in the back of the arena and a great view of the band. When I asked what he was looking at, he told me, "The tunnel. Don't tell me you don't see it."

It took me a few minutes to figure out that he was staring at one of the Garden's walkways (where the twirlers twirled) leading to the building's lit concourse, imagining the walkway to be a portal to some otherworldly place. I never let him live that down. We would frequently joke about "finding the tunnel," which became a metaphor for everything: "I need to find the tunnel and break out of this batting slump in softball." "Jerry is a little off tonight, he needs to find the tunnel."

On our way to a Meadowlands show in Jersey, Paul and I did "find the tunnel" after missing the exit for the George Washington Bridge. We ended up in Midtown and the Holland Tunnel, which we drove through laughing the whole way as we listened to 2-9-73.

Paul was only 32 when he died, but he had accomplished a lot in his life. He led Mercy College (NY) to back-to-back conference (NYCAC) championships in Division II golf and was NYCAC Player of the Year in his senior season. He became a certified special education teacher who later moved on to a career in finance. He married his college sweetheart, Lynda, who was a softball star at Mercy, and together they had two beautiful daughters.

In the spring of 2017, I heard from Lynda, as I often do. Their youngest daughter was having a Sweet Sixteen party and they were going to honor Paul with a Grateful Dead song. Lynda wanted to know which song would be appropriate; the answer came to me immediately. Without hesitating, I relied, "'Ripple.'"

"I knew you would say that," came her answer.

Once in a while, I still sense Paul's playful presence, shadow boxing over my shoulder, almost always at night. By the time I turn around, he's gone, off to the tunnel, and I'm left alone with my memories and thoughts.

Sometimes at night, I think I understand.

2008

The Grateful Dead supported green organizations such as the Rainforest Action Network, Cultural Survival, and Greenpeace, so it's fitting that Bobby's sister-in-law, Leilani Maaja Münter, is one of the leading eco-athletes in the world.

Leilani is a race car driver and environmental activist who drives for the Venturini Motorsports team in the ARCA Racing Series. In February, 2017, she drove a Vegan Powered-themed car in an ARCA race at Daytona. Ms. Münter, who previously drove in the Firestone Indy Lights (the developmental league of IndyCar), has been ranked by *Sports Illustrated* as one of the top ten female race car drivers in the world.

Tiny Leilani (she's only 5'3"), who grew up in Minnesota, uses a solar-based system in her car's pit area — a carbon-free structure and infrastructure powered by carbon negative fuel. The long-time vegetarian graduated from the University of California-San Diego, where she earned a degree in Biology, specializing in Ecology, Behavior and Evolution.

Convincing NASCAR or any auto racing series, which welcome change as readily as the wealthy embrace tax reform, to adopt, change or even consider more stringent environmental policies is no small feat. Yet, progress is being made by Ms. Münter — NASCAR has officially switched from leaded to unleaded gas, and the IndyCar Series is now using 100 percent ethanol in its cars.

"Everybody wants to get off oil," Leilani told PVSolarReport.com in 2014. "Every time you put a gallon of gas in your car, people realize that a lot of that money is going to OPEC, to bullets and guns that are shot at our soldiers overseas. The reaction of the race crowd is strong to that, the national security threat, the fact that we're giving away dollars to, in some cases, countries that don't like us very much. It hits home when someone has a son [or daughter] overseas fighting in the war."

Münter is highly-respected for speaking her mind on environmental issues. She blogs in the green section of the *Huffington Post* and on the websites Disruptive Women and Medium and writes for *The Guardian*. In 2008, Leilani became the first Ambassador for the National Wildlife Federation, that same year going to Capitol Hill to speak with members of Congress on behalf of the Climate Security Act. Four years later, Münter spoke at a rally on Capitol Hill, again in support of the CSA, along with senators Barbara Boxer, John Kerry and Joe Lieberman.

In 2010, Leilani, who resides in North Carolina, was chosen by the Planet Green Network as the No. 1 Eco Athlete in the world and was also featured in the network's series, "Fast Forward," which spotlights environmental heroes. In 2012, *Glamour Magazine* named her one of its "Eco Heroes" and *ELLE Magazine* rewarded her efforts with its Genius Award.

Of corporate sponsorship, Münter told Midweek.com, "Because I am so involved in the environmental world, I don't just take money from anybody. I vet each sponsor I am working with to ensure their environmental practices are solid. I can't bring my environmental message to the 100 million racing fans in America and feel OK about it if I am doing it with a company that is not being responsible with the environment."

As Leilani told PVSolarReport: "It doesn't matter what your background is or where you're from — we all can make decisions every day that are helping the planet or not."

Bobby has been an ardent supporter of Leilani, attending one of her ARCA series races at Daytona International Speedway in Florida. During a podcast from TRI in 2016, Leilani asked Bobby how he first became aware of environmental issues. He answered that, after witnessing industrial pollution in a parkland as a child, he formulated a simple approach: "How are humans interfacing with nature, and what looks right and what looks wrong ?"

Ms. Münter believes she can change both the racing world and the planet, warning, "Never underestimate a vegetarian hippie chick with a race car."

2013

"Spots of Time" is an exciting song collaboration between Phil and Warren Haynes that nicks a riff from the Grateful Dead's "Help on the Way." The tune appears on the 2015 Haynes album, *Ashes & Dust*, which features the new grass jamband Railroad Earth serving as Warren's backing outfit.

The composition was written by Phil and Warren in 2013, which is when Haynes began performing the song live with the Allman Brothers Band. "We were in the studio together doing something and Phil told me he had this music that he'd like me to write lyrics to," Warren told *Relix*. "I think what came out was wonderful."

The term "spots of time" is taken from a line in a William Wordsworth poem from 1888 titled "The Prelude." According to academician Jonathan Bishop, "At the center of our experience of 'The Prelude'

are those 'spots of time' where Wordsworth is endeavoring to express key moments in the history of his imagination."

Wordsworth writes in "The Prelude":

There are in our existence spots of time,
That with distinct pre-eminence retain
A renovating virtue

In the song "Spots of Time," Warren beautifully articulates the same sentiment as Wordsworth — that time moves swiftly ahead and it's OK to hold onto the memories and images of our past; in fact, it's essential:

Spots of time flash before my eyes
Like ribbons of light
Helplessly I try to touch them
Before they disappear into the night

Do you remember
How young we were or is it just me
Imagining like I always do
When we were once wild and free

A longing for days past and reflecting on years gone by are common themes in our life as we age and a fixture in Robert Hunter's lyrics:

This is all a dream we dreamed
one afternoon long ago

April 18, 2015

When professional golfer Jim Furyk won his 17th career PGA Tour title in April, 2015, the winning caddie was his long-time sideman, Michael "Fluff" Cowan, an avowed Deadhead and a 40-year PGA veteran. Cowan's renown as a Grateful Dead fan exploded after he was pictured wearing a T-shirt with a colorful Jerry image on it in a 1997 *Sports Illustrated* article on golfer Tiger Woods. "I think so much of the band and their music and what it [means] to me," he was quoted as saying in the piece.

At the Masters that same year, Fluff looped for Woods during his record-shattering victory, wearing a different Grateful Dead-themed T-shirt under his white jumpsuit for each round.

Mike is one of the best-known sports personalities (along with Bill Walton, Tim Flannery and Joe Maddon) to unabashedly call themselves a Deadhead. Fluff is so old school that he still listens to his Maxell and TDK tapes. "I still have a reasonable collection of live tapes, and I still listen a lot, and, I'd have to say, I'll always be a Deadhead," he says.

The Maine native, who has caddied in eleven Ryder Cups and will likely have a role in the 2018 competition with Furyk having been appointed team captain, has wins in two major championships on his resume. One of the tour's most respected bagmen, Cowan has caddied for Ed Sabo (1976–78), Peter Jacobsen (1978–96), Woods (1996–99) and Furyk (1999–present).

The affable Fluff recalls with fondness the time he worked for Tiger: "Watching him win a major in his first year was wonderful … like being in the front row at a Grateful Dead show."

Not that Cowan ever got Woods to kick back and listen to the Dead. "I would have liked Tiger to listen to it, to understand it," he says. "But when you get right down to it, it doesn't really matter if he did or if he didn't."

In retrospect, maybe Tiger should have opened an ear.

Fluff was on Furyk's bag when he shot a PGA Tour-record score of 58 — ten birdies and an eagle — during the final round of the Travelers Championship in August, 2016. That's more improbable than hearing your twelve favorite Grateful Dead songs in the same show and just as cool !

Is there anything Fluff has learned as a Deadhead that has contributed to his success as a caddie ? "Just go with the flow !" he answers with a smile as he flips the 90-minute TDK tape in his cassette player.

Spring, 2015

A guy walks into a bar and hears three kids playing a Grateful Dead song in an empty back room …

Sounds like the beginning of another bar joke until the guy turns out to be Billy and the kids an aspiring rock band."

In New Orleans to play gigs with 7 Walkers and Dead Feat (Paul Barrere and Fred Tackett of Little Feat, guitarist Anders Osborne, and Bill) and soak in the night life during the spring of 2015, the fun-loving Kreutzmann couldn't help but to notice the music coming from the back. "I heard a band playing 'Scarlet Begonias,'" he wrote on Twitter. "I couldn't help myself. I just had to play it with them. The drummer handed me his sticks and I jammed it out with the young bassist and guitarist.

"Afterwards, they freaked out about how much fun it was and they asked me my name. When I told them who I was … well … it was a pretty special moment. But it was before then — when I first got behind their drums and played my first beat with these strangers … young kids trying on a song that I had the honor of playing around the world … that the joy in my eyes lit up."

After Weir landed a job as a guitar instructor at Dana Morgan Music with Garcia's help early in 1964, the two met an aspiring drummer who had been kicked out of his school band for being unable to keep a beat. The drummer's more sympathetic parents encouraged their son to stay with it and arranged for him to take lessons at Dana Morgan, the foundation for the musical relationship between Garcia and Weir and Bill.

"Today was one of those days when I was reminded of just how much of a joy and a privilege it is to make music with people," Billy tweeted.

"Thank you, New Orleans. Never change."

And you never change as well, Mr. Kreutzmann !

July 3, 2015

Backstage in his private practice space, Bobby's sporting a pair of wire-rimmed glasses and beat-up Birkenstocks as he picks at his guitar prior to opening night of the Dead's three 50th anniversary shows in Chicago. There's an empty chair to his left, no doubt placed there by Mr. Weir in anticipation of Garcia, or his spirit, showing up for a pre-gig duet.

And, should Jerry's apparition have appeared, acoustic guitar in hand, Bobby would have been neither surprised nor unprepared. Maybe just a little pissed off: "Where you been, big brother ? I been waiting on you."

"Watching over you, baby brother."

On the cabinet to Bobby's left is a setlist for tonight's show, held in place by a metallic Steal Your Face magnet; to the right is a tiny American flag. There's a host of stickers on the cabinet, the most amusing of which is white with purple lettering and reads: Make Bobby Shave.

A red, white and blue Stealie and a TRI sticker can also be spotted, as can a bumper sticker that one might assume contains Weir's guiding life principle: Mischief Is Bliss.

To his right, a cabinet hosts three guitars. Its wall is adorned with pins and photos, one containing two images of Bobby onstage — one more recent, the other from his Dead days.

Just minutes from showtime, Mr. Weir's demeanor suggests he's contented and at peace with the road that has brought him here. Like all the great ones, he appears relaxed, focused and prepared, exuding the quiet confidence of a great athlete — think Roger Federer — sitting in front of his locker, knowing he's about to secure another Wimbledon title.

July 3, 2015 II

After Garcia's passing and the disbandment of the Grateful Dead, Bobby and Phil became the torchbearers of the band's flame.

But by the time the Dead's reunion shows in Santa Clara and Chicago rolled around in the summer of 2015, it was Phil who arrived holding the mantelpiece of the Grateful Dead's legacy, having edged Mr. Weir by a nose.

Bobby had recently fought, and lost, battles with his health (shoulder), the road, and the trappings of the road, proving he was as frail and human as you and I.

In the summer of 2014, during RatDog's tour of the Southwest and West Coast, Weir hit the skids, culminating with a Hunter S. Thompson-esque evening in Vegas, where members of RatDog prohibited him from going onstage. Thirty minutes before showtime, Bobby was seen tossing back shots and drinking beers with fans at the casino bar; moments before he was scheduled to go on, he sat alone, chugging King Louis XIII cognac, valued at $2,000 a bottle, straight from the bottle.

Who hasn't sat around a bar or some shithole guzzling King Louie or some other gut rot, getting hammered, alone, and in a dark place ?

Garcia played a major role in validating Weir's life, and Bobby may never come to terms with Jerry's death. When you're the on-stage yin to a musical genius' yang, and that person's best and most loyal friend, it's life affirming. Playing sideman was egoless and mostly thankless work for Bob and he did it for 30 years, honestly and humbly, because he knew it made both Jerry and the Grateful Dead better.

Mr. Lesh, along with promoter Peter Shapiro, were able to dictate the terms of the reunion: there would only be three shows (later expanded to five), Trey Anastasio would be the lead guitarist, and there would be no on-stage joint appearances by the Core Four before or after the reunion. (At the "Dear Jerry" concert at the Merriweather Post Pavilion in April, 2015, the four, all present, not only did not perform together, they didn't even pose for a single photo together.)

Phil and Shapiro then shoved those terms down the throats of Weir, Kreutzmann and Hart.

And our throats as well.

In fairness, Phil wanted no part of a large-scale tour for health reasons and because, blessedly, he did not need the money. Shapiro knew that a limited number of shows would maximize ticket and merchandising profits and all but guarantee a sharp, focused band, an exuberant crowd, and an exciting environment.

When Phil and Bobby arrived at the reunion shows the two were no longer friends, an animosity that had been smoldering for more than two years, the result of Weir's fall at the Capitol in April, 2013, the cancellation of Furthur headlining gigs at festivals in 2013 and 2014, and the debacle in Vegas.

"Me and Phil, we're cool, I'll play with him anytime," Billy privately told Shapiro in May, 2015. "But Bobby and Phil, they're done."

July 4, 2015

The Hug.

It came early in the first set of the July 4 show on Saturday night at Soldier Field. The Dead had just played an exuberant "Liberty" and there were good tidings in the air. However, the enmity between Weir and Lesh was clearly evident onstage during the first three gigs of this historic five-show farewell. To diffuse that tension, Phil walked over to Bobby and gave him a hug, a big hug, and Bob hugged him right back. It was cool, what a more-caustic voice might term a Hallmark Moment, and much needed.

"Standing on the Moon," one of Hunter's finest pieces of literature, followed. The song was one of Jerry's showstoppers and tonight it served the same purpose. Beautifully sung by Trey, whose voice doesn't quite have the resonance that Garcia's had, the *Built to Last* track was delivered with grace and tact.

"Me and My Uncle" was the most-played song in the performing history of the Grateful Dead, so you know Bobby had to bring out the old warhorse one last time. (Whenever I hear the "I'm as honest as a Denver man can be" line, I always think of Neal Cassady, who spent part of his youth in Denver.) The opening notes to "Tennessee Jed" followed, triggering a wave of ecstasy among the 60,000 faithful. Trey drew out, and nailed, the bridge solo, slowly building its momentum until the band and Deadheads were storming the gates of delirium.

Next, "Cumberland Blues" burned like the Great Chicago Fire of 1871, while "Little Red Rooster" paid homage to the home of the blues. "Friend of the Devil" was true to the *American Beauty* version, followed by a lengthy, super-charged "Deal," bringing set one to a close.

The second set was a Murderer's Row of heavy hitters led off by Phil, who sang a lengthy and jammed-out "Bird Song." One of the evening's highlights came next — a rip-roaring "The Golden Road (to Unlimited Devotion)," sung by Trey, who tore up those Garcia riffs.

There was no stopping this psychedelic septet now ! Weir took front-and-center for a magical trek through "Lost Sailor", "Saint of Circumstance." He was powerful, centered, and commanding, the rock star we have loved since he was a baby-faced teen. Another great moment followed: Hornsby singing "West L.A. Fadeaway," one of Garcia and Hunter's bleakest tunes, a noir novella about the unseemly side of life. Bruce knew Jerry well, and Garcia respected and appreciated Hornsby, who was all too familiar with the pain Jerry lived with. Hornsby's vocals captured, and reflected, that pain.

Trey's take on "Foolish Heart" set the sails for the land of enchantment, casting our souls to sea. His singing and playing was filled with a high-flying, positive energy.

Great sports teams have a set of role players they can rely on game in and game out to show up and put in a yeoman's effort. Role players grind it out, mostly anonymously, and rarely steal the spotlight from the superstars. That's the role Mickey and Billy filled in the Grateful Dead for three decades. In Santa Clara and ChiTown, to no one's surprise, the duo were their typically-reliable selves, able to take their solo to new and, as always, captivating places. Mickey coaxed sounds out of the Beam, an eight-foot aluminum instrument featuring 13 bass piano strings tuned to the chord of D, that were not of this world.

There was a humorous moment during the drum solo. As Hart worked the Beam, he was maddeningly gesturing like Leonard Bernstein conducting the New York Philharmonic. When Phil walked by, he stopped in front of Mickey and began to conduct alongside the drum master.

It made both Mickey and Phil crack up.

A protracted and far, far-out "space" led to a stunning "Stella Blue," sung by Weir. Anastasio did a superb job on the exit solo.

Way to go, Phish guy !

"One More Saturday" rocked us home.

In Manhattan on the night of July 4, the lights on the Empire State Building were synchronized to the Dead's live performance of the "U.S. Blues" encore by Empire State lighting designer Marc Brickman, who created the visual and technical design of the music-to-light show featuring Grateful Dead images and icons.

Was "the Hug" nothing more than a symbolic gesture ? An attempt to put aside, for a day, the ill will between Phil and Bobby ?

Likely.

Will time heal this wound ?

I'm certain.

July 5, 2015

How did Trey Anastasio so successfully fill the role of lead guitarist for the Dead's five reunion shows that two weeks after the final concert, Anastasio had Deadheads clamoring for more (a sentiment shared by Billy) ?

Trey brought the necessary ingredients to the band the way Earl "the Pearl" Monroe brought his full arsenal of basketball skills to the New York Knicks after his acquisition in a trade with the Baltimore Bullets before the 1972-73 season. The Pearl was a gifted, and flashy, All Star who arrived in the Big Apple with a fresh, team-oriented attitude, the willingness to forsake individual goals for team accomplishments, and, like Anastasio, the desire to be a part of something great, ultimately helping to lead the Knickerbockers to the NBA title in '73.

Like the Pearl, Trey brought a key intangible to the Dead: confidence. He believes he can play at any level, with anyone, and in any situation. Anastasio knew when to lay back and when to step forward, knocking down one big shot after another, setting up his teammates for easy baskets, and making thrilling play after thrilling play.

Trey came rehearsed and fully-committed: He added effects to his guitar to better achieve the "Jerry sound," practiced with Bobby and Phil both individually and as a trio, and even went so far as to listen to his attic-stored live Grateful Dead cassette tapes. As the old saying goes: Not preparing to win is preparing to lose.

There was no way Anastasio was going to fail.

Trey's greatest accomplishment over the course of the five shows was allowing the band to be a band again, as they were when Jerry was alive, and allowing us, newcomers and veterans alike, to experience, and re-visit, special feelings, places and times.

There were several outstanding incarnations of the Grateful Dead involving the Core Four following Jerry's passing: the Other Ones in 2002; the Dead in 2009, and Furthur. But no post-Garcia band approached the essence of the Grateful Dead as successfully as the Anastasio-led version of the Dead.

Whether you were at the reunion concerts or couch-surfing at home, what we remember best about the five shows is the emotion: the overwhelming sense of happiness that infiltrated every nook and cranny and permeated everyone — the band, Deadheads and music fans.

Pearl brought moxie, which he could back up on the court, to the Knicks. Trey brought the same pluck to the Dead. His confidence spoke to the fact he had seemingly spent a lifetime preparing for this moment.

Like the Pearl, only Trey could have taken an already great team and made them better.

And that is a true sign of greatness.

Fall, 2015

Before embarking on the first Dead & Company tour in the fall of 2015, John Mayer delivered this simple message via Twitter: "This was the Grateful Dead recording that sold me."

Mayer selected a *Dick's Picks* featuring two shows from one of the band's most-respected performing eras. But more on that later.

First, some background on Mayer, who has been nominated for nineteen Grammy Awards, winning seven, including one for "Waiting on the World to Change" in 2007. John has released just seven studio albums since 2001, the most recent being *The Search for Everything* (2017). He owns an extensive cache of watches and guitars, with his watch collection valued at north of $10 million and his guitar stash numbering more than 200. He has collaborated with both Martin Guitars and Fender to design signature acoustic guitars and electric Stratocasters.

Like the Grateful Dead, Mayer is involved with philanthropy and charity. His "Back to You" foundation benefits health care, education, arts and talent programs. On his webpage, there's a link that details his work with the Northern California Institute for Research and Education, a San Francisco-based organization that provides services to combat veterans. NCIRE arranges for Mayer to meet and speak with vets as they return home from deployments. "No two people or experiences are exactly the same," notes Mayer on his page. "But the fundamental message is clear: respect ... and show care."

In the early 2010s, the Montana resident found refuge in both Big Sky country and the music of the Grateful Dead after his regrettable remarks in a February, 2010 interview with *Playboy* turned his life upside down. During this time, he recorded the introspective pieces *Born and Raised* (2012) and *Paradise Valley* (2013), had a granuloma removed from his vocal chords, and tweeted he was "interested in getting into the Grateful Dead" but didn't "know where to begin."

In September, 2015, the guitarist demonstrated he had found a jumping-off point by posting a link to *Dick's Picks, Vol. 29*, the two-show set that "sold" him on the Dead. This four-CD collection is composed of a May 19, 1977 concert at the Fox Theater in Atlanta and a May 21, 1977 gig at the Civic Center Arena in Lakeland, Florida.

It's gratifying to know that Mayer dove into our tie-dyed pool based on a set of shows from one of the Grateful Dead's most-celebrated live eras.

October 1, 2015

Luke Walton is the son of NBA Hall of Famer and renowned Deadhead Bill Walton, a former-college All-American at the University of Arizona, a veteran of seven NBA seasons spent with the Lakers and Cavs, and a Deadhead himself (he famously has a White Lightning Man tattoo on his right bicep). In 2010, Luke and his father became the first father and son to have won multiple NBA championships: Bill won rings in 1977 (with Portland) and 1986 (Boston) and Luke in 2009 and 2010 (both with the Lakers).

On October 1, 2015, Luke was named interim head coach of the reigning world champion Golden State Warriors. Under Walton's tutelage, the Warriors began the season with a 24–0 record, the longest undefeated start to the start of a season in the history of professional sports. When head coach Steve Kerr returned to the bench, Golden State had a 39-4 mark with Luke at the helm, matching the record of the 1995-96 Chicago Bulls through 43 games.

Walton was named head coach of the Los Angeles Lakers on April 29, 2016, the 26th coach in franchise history. He faces a tall task. The Lakers finished with a 26-56 record in Luke's first year, a modest but respectable nine-win improvement from the previous season, but the team's front office is in disarray. Ownership is banking on Magic Johnson and Luke to return the franchise to its storied past.

The younger Walton, like his father, won as a college and NBA player. But, unlike Bill, Luke was not a superstar on the professional level. He was a role player during the Phil Jackson-coached and Kobe Bryant-led championship years in Los Angeles. Like back-up catchers in baseball, who tend to make good managers in the majors because of the perspective offered by their proximity in the dugout to the manager's maneuverings, Luke's front-row seat to Jackson's coaching brilliance will eventually help him get to Terrapin !

October 19, 2015

Phil is, and always has been, a battler and a survivor.

With his recent announcement that he has bladder cancer, Mr. Lesh is facing yet another battle, one of several health issues he has endured in the past 15-plus years. In September, 1998, he suffered an internal hemorrhage, the result of a chronic hepatitis C infection first diagnosed in March, 1998, undergoing a liver transplant in late 1998.

Since then, Phil has served as a ceaseless advocate for registering people as organ donors. At his concerts, he honors the life and spirit of Cody, the young man whose liver he received, by wearing a sweatband with the name "Cody" on it and by telling fans to "turn to someone that you love, and loves you, and knows you well, and say, 'Hey, if anything ever happens to me, I want to be an organ donor.'"

This is the second time Phil has fought cancer. In October, 2006, he revealed he had been diagnosed with prostate cancer, the illness that claimed his dad's life. That December, he underwent successful prostate surgery.

If you could use the word "fortunate" to describe being diagnosed with any type of cancer, bladder cancer has, fortunately, a very high survival rate. The website cancer.org defines "survival rate" as "the percentage of patients who live at least five years after their cancer is diagnosed." Per the National Cancer Institute's SEER database, with early diagnosis, the survival rate for bladder cancer is 98 percent.

For more than 15 years, Mr. Lesh has colored Phil and Friends with diverse lineups that often served as break-out moments for artists such as Jackie Greene, Eric Krasno, Derek Trucks, Scott Law, Stu Allen and Nicki Bluhm. In all, there have been approximately 60 different members of Phil and Friends since 1998, representing almost every known and unknown artist and band from the jamband world and beyond, a testament to Lesh's musical ear and vision.

If someone had told me in the Seventies or Eighties that, one day, Phil would not only have a solo band but that you would be able to see his band regularly and that they would interpret the music of the Grateful Dead in fun and interesting ways, I would have had a hard time believing you. Mr. Lesh was the guy who mostly, and superbly, played bass in the shadow of Jerry and Bob.

Thirty years of the Dead may not have been an eternity but it was long enough for any Deadhead to recognize the band was not just unique but highly singular in both music and life. Phil, in his own right, has become equally singular, a national treasure to be cherished as well as our ambassador to the jamband, music and straight worlds.

October 31, 2015

The crown jewel of the newly-renovated Madison Square Garden is The Bridge, two parallel catwalks high above the Garden floor that provide phenomenal seating and breathtaking views. On Saturday night, a dream setlist, a stunning display of musicianship, and the usual highly-supportive New York crowd allowed Dead & Company to turn the mammoth Seventh Avenue shrine into an intimate downtown club.

Having spent weeks in rehearsal, these six world-class musicians are in peak form just two dates into a national tour, performing effortlessly and without ego while interpreting and honoring the music of the Grateful Dead. Effortlessly, that is, but not without high-octane energy, from the brief jam that led into the "Jack Straw" opener until the closing notes of "Werewolves of London."

It was a heart-tug to hear John Mayer, one of the young guns who will accompany the Grateful Dead's music into the future, sing Jerry's lines with such valor on "Jack Straw." The bridges between the song's verses were drawn out, and the mid-section solo, one of the many staples that affirmed Garcia's six-string greatness, was capably handled by Mayer. The real power during John's solo was generated by the band behind him, a herd of rampaging elephants stampeding across the Serengeti with sound and fury. Adding to the thunder: Jeff Chimenti's piano, rewarded here with a huge Garden hand. Chimenti should buy a few lottery tickets — it's been his good fortune to have been a member of every hip Grateful Dead off-shoot band in the past two-plus decades: RatDog, the Dead, Furthur, Phil and Friends and, now, Dead & Co.

"New Speedway Boogie," sung by Weir, was tailor-made for the gritty, blues stylings of Mayer, who conjured some of the darkness embedded in the song's DNA by Garcia and Hunter. John sang "Brown-Eyed Woman" with a passion that makes it clear he has drank from the Kool-Aid, able to go deep inside the pocket because he has taken the time, individually and with the other members of Dead & Co., to learn the Grateful Dead's music. And he became familiar with it no differently than you or I — someone turned him onto a tape, he began to listen and get into the music and Jerry's magical guitar ... and the next thing you know, he's having the entire *Dick's Picks* and *Dave's Picks* catalogs Fed Ex-ed overnight.

However, unlike nearly all of us, Mayer could pick up a guitar and chase after the notion of seeing how well he could emulate Garcia's unique style. Early in 2015, Bobby was a guest on "The Late Late Show" hosted by Mayer. The pair performed a perfunctory "Truckin'" but when Mayer tore it up on "Althea," the idea of working together was hatched.

"Ramble on Rose" always worked well at the Garden and Saturday night was no different; the song's cadence matches the march of Manhattan, its lyrics capture the circus of its streets, and the "just like New York City" line still elicits a big cheer. The crowd was eager to shower the band with applause and, following a deep solo on "Althea," Mayer had to take a step back as he approached the mic because of the voracious hand he received, and earned, for his prowess. He played the living daylights out of "Althea," repeating the line "and forgetting the love we bring" three times before launching into the song's conclusion.

Mayer blew up the various "Cassidy" solo sections while leading the song down a musical side street during its ecliptic bridge. John excitedly let loose a loud *"Whoo !"* as he steered the group through a piece (clearly worked on in rehearsals) that blended reggae, walking blues and rock and roll. What is the guitarist hoping to accomplish onstage ? "Finding an authentic space between how I play the guitar and what my instincts are and what these songs are at their core," he told *Billboard*.

"Deal," sung by Mayer, brought a stout end to set one. The houselights rose and a New York Mets' logo was being projected in the "brain section" of the Skull and Roses stage prop serving as a video screen. (Just a five-iron away in Queens, the Mets were duking it out against the Kansas City Royals in Game 4 of the World Series.)

The Garden crowd, long the X Factor propelling the home team to greatness inside the World's Most Famous Arena, was at a hyper-excited level, unleashing unconditional love on the band at every turn. The second set started with a jam that led into "Truckin'," which slid nicely into "Wang Dang Doodle." The reliable one-two of "Estimated Prophet", "Eyes of the World" followed. Bobby looked amazing, in great physical shape and as handsome as ever; his hair was smartly styled, he sported a thick handlebar mustache and wore a black T-shirt, grey Capris and sandals. Mayer's guitar work throughout "Eyes of the World" was near-letter perfect, an absolute credit to his preparation. Weir sang "Eyes," expertly

capturing the vocal lilt of the song, another tune that featured extended jams between verses. Toward the end of the *Wake of the Flood* masterpiece, the band laid back and allowed bassist Oteil Burbridge (Aquarium Rescue Unit, Allman Brothers Band) to freelance during an extended solo, another example of why this band will kill it nightly.

Dead & Co. brought out the heavy artillery in set two, a Willy's in four-wheel drive engaging in a reciprocal energy exchange with the throng of 20,000. An electric current jolted the crowd as Mayer began to play the introductory chords to "Terrapin Station." John seemed awed by the response. He sang the opening verses, his voice strong and confident, a young gun tackling Hunter's magnificent tale and Garcia's opus. A fever pitch was being achieved as Mayer sang verse after verse, especially with his soulful reading of the lyrics: "Since the end is never told, we pay the teller off in gold in hopes he will come back/ He cannot be bought or sold." The excitement in the audience began to peak as the band approached the "Inspiration, move me brightly !" declaration, knowing Bobby would be taking over the vocals. When Weir delivered, the Garden thunder became the evening's highlight and its most-emotional moment, as thrilling as going over the first descent on a roller coaster.

Mickey and Billy maintained a steady rhythm during their drum solo that evolved into another hypnotic performance by Hart on the Beam, which he plays, at times, using a bow. The pair wore Halloween costumes during their solo: Hart sported a red cape with a large, cuffed collar that definitely put the devil in Rhythm Devil !

A brief "space" interlude, featuring the full band, followed, during which Mayer, in tandem with Weir, admirably did his best to create some cosmic noodlings. What followed from here was a triumphant closing run: "China Cat Sunflower", "I Know You, Rider", "Morning Dew", "One More Saturday Night."

Bang ! as Villanova basketball coach Jay Wright would say.

Mayer was, deservedly, later feted by *Billboard* as "masterful."

After returning to the stage, Weir, John and Oteil began to howl into their mics, prompting the crowd to howl right back. Dead & Co. launched into Warren Zevon's "Werewolves of London," a fun moment in an evening of fun, and powerful, moments.

November 4, 2015

Phil and Bobby's "hug" during the first set of the Dead's show on July 4 in Chicago was mostly a symbolic gesture, as genuine as Bill Belichick and Rex Ryan wrapping their arms around each other. However, four months later — on November 4 — Phil and Bobby shared a second, and far different, on-stage hug.

That night, during a late-night performance by Grahame Lesh's band, Midnight North, at the Sounds of Brazil in Soho, Phil and Bobby jumped onstage to play together for the first time since the Dead's final show on July 5. It was also the first time the pair had seen each other since Phil's recovery from bladder surgery.

They hugged mightily. Not the "bro hug" they exchanged in Chicago but a genuine, heart-felt hug that took the two back to their first meeting in Palo Alto in April, 1965, when life was much simpler and the possibilities, though daunting, infinite.

After Jerry passed away, Phil and Bobby became brothers, bonded by their grief and desire to perpetuate the Grateful Dead's music and culture. Like Ray and Dave Davies, Chris and Rich Robinson, Noel and Liam Gallagher, and Mick and Keith, Lesh and Weir have had their share of disagreements and fallings out since 1995.

And no different than the Davies boys and the Glimmer Twins, Bob and Phil have always managed to patch things up, move on, and get back to the music. To wit: Weir joined the bassist and the Terrapin Family Band on March 6, 2017 at Terrapin Crossroads, where they opened the second set with a Phil-sung "New Potato Caboose" (on *Anthem of the Sun*, the song is sung by Weir), "Born Cross-Eyed" — just as the songs are paired on *Anthem* ! Bobby and Phil have also announced they will be playing together again with the Family Band on August 26 at the Lockin' Festival.

Over the past two-plus decades, a lot of water has passed under the bridge between the two brothers.

If Bob and Phil have learned anything since Jerry's passing, it's this: Life is short and getting shorter, forgiveness is the key to every door, and love does not fade away.

November 27, 2015

How well have Dead & Company meshed heading into the final two shows of their first national tour ?

So well that John Mayer took Oteil, Billy and other members of the band and crew on a tour of Medicine Man, one of Colorado's largest marijuana cultivation facilities. "It was awesome — it was so much fun," Andy Williams, the CEO of Medicine Man, told TheCannabist.com. "You should have seen John Mayer when he took that one picture (in the photo, Mayer is seen in a Zen stance, surrounded by plants in a grow room) — I was standing right behind the camera person, and they were having so much fun in there."

Suffice to say, Dead & Co. are having the same level of fun onstage.

Mayer, Billy and Oteil turned their sight-seeing tour through Medicine Man into a leisurely stroll. "When we first got in there, they were very conscious of pictures being taken and wanted this to be their time," said Williams. "So, we got them in the back pretty quickly and started showing them around. We never let anybody in our rooms but for these guys, you open the doors.

"We let them spend as much time and ask as many questions as they wanted. We took them through the veg rooms and through different flower rooms, we showed them the different stages of growth, two different cure rooms, and the trim room."

I want to visit the Trim Room disguised as the Invisible Man, invisible Hefty Bag in hand.

Mayer & Co. swapped a bunch of backstage passes with the Medicine Man staff in exchange for some of the facility's gear. The bartering of any other "goods" is purely speculative ! Williams also gave the band a custom-built drum as a gift for Mickey, who didn't attend the tour because, of course, he had been there before, been there before ...

December 6, 2015

Bobby has set to work on a solo album — *Blue Mountain* — composed of "cowboy songs" and has reached out to John Barlow, his long-time lyricist.

A visibly thinner and healthier-looking Mr. Barlow, who is recovering from a debilitating heart attack suffered on May 27 of this year, posted a photograph of himself on Moby Picture flanked by Bob and Lukas Nelson, a member of Promise of the Real and the son of country music legend Willie Nelson. He captioned the photo with these words: "Three Wise Men came together to write a cowboy song today. We, Lukas Autry Nelson, Bobby Weir and I, got a start."

Given the task at hand, it's fitting Lukas Nelson's middle name is Autry, which Willie selected to honor Gene Autry, the famed "Singing Cowboy" who ruled the country music, film and radio worlds from the Thirties on.

Weir has been searching high and low for songwriting partners, reaching out to Mr. Barlow, Nelson, Joe Russo (Furthur, JRAD) and members of both the National and the Yellowbirds. Eventually, Bobby began to write and record with Idaho-native Josh Ritter (Royal City Band) and Brooklynite Josh Kaufman (Yellowbirds).

Barlow began writing lyrics for Weir compositions in 1971. In February of that year, he rekindled his friendship with Bobby backstage at the Capitol Theatre in Port Chester. "Weir figured that since I was a poet, I ought to be able to write lyrics," recalls Barlow, who graduated from Wesleyan University in 1969 with high honors in comparative religion (he also studied poetry). "We started around early '71."

During longs nights fueled by Wild Turkey, the two began a prolific songwriting period in their partnership. "There was a depth of feeling on both our parts," recalls Barlow.

Even though the much-hoped-for songwriting reunion between Bob and Mr. Barlow hasn't panned out yet, as the lyricist is still attending to his health issues, it was great to see the pair reunited.

December 31, 2015

When did John Mayer and Bobby first think they might have something ?

At the soundcheck for Weir's guest appearance on "The Late Late Show" in January, 2015.

It didn't take long for Bob to realize he had a special chemistry with Mayer. "The soundcheck was almost impossible to stop," he recalls. "It just occurred, and the clouds parted. That's when I knew we [might have] a band. We had the kind of fun that you just don't walk away from.

"It was not unlike the night I met Jerry on New Year's Eve of [1963]."

Bobby is referring to the first extended meeting between him and Garcia, on New Year's Eve 1963 at Dana Morgan Music in Palo Alto. "I was walking around the backstreets of Palo Alto with one of the guys in my group and we walked past the back of Dana Morgan Music and heard banjo music coming from inside," reminisces Bob. "It was Garcia, waiting for his students to show up, at a loss as to why none of his students were there."

Dead & Co. have demonstrated amazing on-stage chemistry. "It's telepathy," Bobby observed. "We're not thinking; we're just letting it pour out. John fits in perfectly."

"It's the most incredible thing," adds Mickey. "We just need to stand in a small circle and look at each other."

Mayer had an unlikely mentor — Trey Anastasio. The pair spent time in Chicago during the Dead's reunion shows. "Trey started talking about how much charisma Jerry had." One of their conversations took place backstage during the drum solo. "They kept telling [Trey] he had to go back onstage."

Another mentor was Weir, who told Mayer if he wanted to familiarize himself with the Grateful Dead, he should immerse himself in shows from 1977 and the spring, 1990 tour. "I'm still shaking," says Mayer. "'77 is the most approachable era. But then you go back to '72 or '73, where they're in a much more raw state, and my favorite version [of the Grateful Dead] becomes 'Strat-era Jerry.' All of a sudden, I go: 'Oh, he's a blues guy !' He's basically doing Freddie King licks, but he's bending them better than all the legends."

Why does Mr. Mayer love performing the songs of the Grateful Dead ? "The music keeps changing ... you can't predict or map it.

"I don't feel pressure, but I feel a responsibility."

Does John think he has been successful ? "I think I [have served as a] conduit to take you to that place you used to go."

January 10, 2016

Since David Bowie's passing on January 10, 2016, just two days after his 69th birthday and the release of his 28th and final studio album, *Blackstar*, fans continue to analyze and dissect the LP. They search for meaning, profound or otherwise, hoping to learn a life lesson or garner a message from a man, who, given the perspective of imminent death and the enlightenment that comes with it, might have some wisdom to pass along.

Ultimately, the songs on *Blackstar* have come to be held in the same light as the songs recorded by the Grateful Dead prior to Garcia's passing (among them, "Lazy River Road" and "So Many Roads") — sage musings on mortality, the purpose and breadth of life, and the passing of time.

SET TWO

Let's examine what Mr. Bowie and Mr. Garcia each had to say in parting.

Bowie knew he was dying when he began to record *Blackstar* in January, 2015. His long-time producer, Tony Visconti, would later note in a Facebook post: "He made *Blackstar* for us, his parting gift. I knew for a year this was the way it would be. I wasn't, however, prepared for it."

It has always been my belief that Jerry, in the last year or two of his life, was intuitively aware of his imminent passing. Hunter had this to say about the last time he spoke with Garcia: "He called me a week or two before he died and started complimenting me, which is something he never did. He said, 'Your words never stuck in my throat.' I thought, 'Jerry ? Are you OK ?' — because we took each other utterly for granted for decades. He definitely was saying goodbye and it was the last time we ever spoke."

As he faced death, "[Bowie] was singing very passionately," notes progressive jazz saxophonist Donny McCaslin, who played on *Blackstar*, "and [with] a lot of conviction."

Garcia, as best his frail body and wounded spirit allowed, played and sang with equal passion and conviction to the end.

The pervasive imagery in the *Blackstar* album — light, darkness, mortality, resurrection and the celestial world — are themes also found in the music of the Grateful Dead. It is interesting to note that both the Bowie song "Blackstar" and the Grateful Dead's "Dark Star" each foretell a cataclysmic celestial event — "Dark star crashes ... the forces tear loose from the axis."

The song "Blackstar" and Garcia and Hunter's final masterpiece, "Days Between," also share a common theme: There is a single, lit candle representing hope that will burn for eternity.

Both songs are haunting and beautiful.

In "Blackstar," Bowie sings:

In the villa of Ormen
Stands a solitary candle
At the center of it all
At the center of it all

Mr. Hunter writes in "Days Between":

A hopeful candle lingers
In the land of lullabies
Where headless horsemen vanish
With wild and lonely cries

February 26, 2016

Donna Godchaux was inducted into the Alabama Music Hall of Fame in February, 2016 along with Rolling

Stones' keyboardist and former-Allman Brothers Band member Chuck Leavell, producer Johnny Sandlin, Southern rockers Wet Willie, and session musicians the Muscle Shoals Horns.

Donna earned her reputation as a talented vocalist as a result of her session work at the famed Muscle Shoals Studio in Alabama, backing artists such as Joe Tex and Cher, so it's fitting she entered the Alabama Hall along with the Muscle Shoals Horns.

As Lynyrd Skynyrd wrote: "Muscle Shoals has got the swampers/ And they've been known to pick a song or two/ Lord, they get me off so much/ They pick me up when I'm feeling blue."

Now, how 'bout you ?

This is not the first such honor for Ms. Godchaux — she was inducted into the Rock and Roll Hall of Fame as a member of the Grateful Dead in 1994. Her tenure in the Dead was vastly under-appreciated by many; if Donna was good enough to sing on No. 1 hits by both Elvis Presley and Percy Sledge, then she was good enough for the Grateful Dead.

And she wasn't singing back-up on just any song: Ms. Godchaux sang on Percy Sledge's 1966 chart-topper "When a Man Loves a Woman" and had the remarkable good fortune to sing on Presley's 1969 smash, "Suspicious Minds," the last great single, and final No. 1, from the King.

Donna talked about the experience of singing with Elvis as part of a 2012 interview with the Rock and Roll Hall of Fame + Museum. While living in Florence, Alabama, she unexpectedly received a phone call: "Elvis wants you to come and record on his album."

"It was one of the most amazing events in my life, hearing that I was going to be singing with Elvis Presley," she recalls.

As if she were Jerry standing next to Bill Monroe, Donna was completely star-struck: "Elvis walked into the room and I just went ... {pretends to be unable to speak}. I had never seen a human being that gorgeous in my life."

The session, which took place during the wee hours of the morning (4:00 a.m. to 7:00 a.m.) on January 23, 1969, required eight takes. "He listened to all of our voices individually throughout the whole track," she recalls. "And he was so complimentary and so kind and nice and encouraging. Afterward, we were very calm. {Feigns cool}: 'Thank you, Elvis, we so enjoyed it. This was really fantastic, and thank you for asking us to be on your record.'"

Like Jerry and Robert Hunter, who were both inducted into the Songwriters Hall of Fame in June, 2015, Donna is now a card-carrying member of two prestigious, and honorary, fraternities.

March 21, 2016

On the first day of spring, John Barlow was inducted into the Fountain Valley School Hall of Fame — the prep school in Colorado where John first met a 14-year-old Bob Weir in 1962 — during a ceremony at

Mr. Barlow's Mill Valley home on March 21 attended by Will Webb, a Fountain Valley representative, and Bobby.

Barlow, who graduated from the school in 1965, was presented with a Distinguished Alumni Award while Weir, who managed to get himself expelled from Fountain Valley, did not, understandably and deservedly so, receive any platitudes.

John continues to recover at home from a heart attack. He has been using an Alinker, a revolutionary "walking-bike" described on the Alinker website as an "innovative, non-motorized personal mobility vehicle that enables people to have fun walking on wheels [and to] do more [and] stay independent."

Like many Americans battling health issues, Mr. Barlow's employment insurance benefits only covered so much of the cost of his rehabilitation, another indictment of the American health care system and those who oppose or want to repeal the Affordable Care Act.

By the fall of 2015, Barlow's disability benefits expired and he was overrun by medical bills. "Tragically, even John's healthy savings and robust insurance is no match for the cost of extended convalescence in contemporary America," notes a friend.

A group of musicians, led by Bob, held a fund-raising concert titled "Everyday Miracle: A Benefit for John Perry Barlow" at the Sweetwater Music Hall in Mill Valley on October 24, 2016. Also appearing were Jerry Harrison of the Talking Heads, members of the seminal jamband String Cheese Incident, Sean Lennon and Les Claypool, Lukas Nelson and Ramblin' Jack Elliot.

The John Perry Wellness Trust has been established to help with Mr. Barlow's medical expenses. You can kindly donate any amount to the trust by using this link:

http://www.johnperrybarlow-wellnesstrust.com/

Since May, 1998, the brilliant Barlow has been a fellow at the Harvard Law School's Berkman Center for Internet and Society. When calamity struck, he was serving as a managing partner at Algae Systems, LLC, a Nevada-based energy and utility company he co-founded in 2011 which uses carbon dioxide extracted from the air and algae via carbon capture technology to produce carbon negative fuel.

The Grateful Dead lyricist recently tweeted: "Art is prayer made visible. Music is prayer made audible. Dance is prayer made tangible."

Please keep Mr. Barlow in your prayers as he continues to traverse the highway, the moon, the clouds and the stars on the road to recovery aboard his sleek yellow Alinker.

April 20, 2016

Pearl Jam has canceled tonight's concert in Raleigh, North Carolina, citing the state's recently passed law, HB2, also known as the "bathroom bill," which restricts the access of transgender people to public restrooms, as the reason.

In canceling their North Carolina concert, Eddie Vedder told the crowd at Pearl Jam's show in Hampton on April 18: "The reality is there is nothing like the immense power of boycotting ... it could be the way that ultimately is gonna affect change. We just couldn't find it in ourselves in good conscience to cross a picket line when there was a movement so ..."

As Deadheads, it's imperative we ask ourselves: Should Dead & Company follow the example of Pearl Jam and other major performing artists and organizations such as Bruce Springsteen and the E Street Band, Ringo Starr, Boston and the NCAA and cancel their scheduled show in Charlotte, North Carolina on June 10 at the PNC Music Pavilion ?

Absolutely.

The Grateful Dead never shied away from making political statements and from supporting political actions and causes (not to be confused with supporting politicians).

And now is not the time to start.

Dead & Co. should cancel their Charlotte show on June 10, take whatever financial and PR hit that entails, and move on. Now is no time for Weir & Co. to sell out the ethics, values and principles which have informed our world for 50-plus years.

Life — or call it the intersection of fate and circumstance — has a way of throwing you into the arena when you least expect it. The timing of HB2 and Dead & Company's planned show in North Carolina have unexpectedly thrown the band into the firestorm of one of America's most-heated political issues.

Billy, Bob and Mickey are elder statesmen in the jamband and rock-n-roll worlds. Younger musicians and bands are going to look to them for direction on this issue. Their actions are going to speak loudly to the musicians already out there and the generations to come.

If there was one constant in the Grateful Dead and Deadhead experience, it was this: It's OK to be whomever you are. Our world was, and is, the world where people don't judge, the world where it's safe to comfortably be yourself, the world that is a kind respite from the harsh world around us. LGBTQ people exist in the Grateful Dead world and their fights are real and sadly difficult and have been for a long time.

Not canning the Charlotte show would be an affront to the LGBTQers in the Grateful Dead and Deadhead communities, to all LGBTQ people, and to everyone who faces a fight to be the person they want to be.

On their website, Pearl Jam called the North Carolina law "a despicable piece of legislation that encourages discrimination against an entire group of American citizens."

Ultimately, Dead & Co. did not cancel their show in Charlotte, instead making a $100,000 donation to a local LGBTQ organization — the wealthy call it "throwing money at a problem" — and failing to unite with Pearl Jam, the Boss, the Beatle and other musicians and businesses boycotting North Carolina.

This more-than-egregious mistake by the band and their management company was dictated by a contract that included highly-punitive financial penalties for a cancellation, the result of the Furthur festival cancellations forced by Weir in 2013 and 2014 and his Vegas meltdown in 2014. Bob's unreliability was a major issue when the Dead considered using various promotional companies to back a possible reunion tour or series of shows in 2015, which is one reason they made their bed with, and settled for, Peter Shapiro.

The correct decision for Dead & Co. was to fork over the 100K, cancel the show, and take the financial and PR fastball to the ribs.

May 25, 2016

Phil recently got a chance to cradle an old friend — Tiger !

Jerry's fabled six-string was lent to members of the Grateful Dead and "friends" last week by Jim Irsay.

Chris McKinney, who serves as the curator of Mr. Irsay's vast collection of rare items, accompanied Tiger to San Francisco, where the Core Four became reacquainted with what many consider to be Jerry's most-sacred weapon. In addition to Tiger, Irsay owns guitars from George Harrison and Eric Clapton as well as the original manuscript (a 120-foot typed scroll) of Jack Kerouac's *On the Road*, which Irsay purchased for a whopping $2.46 million in 2001.

Backstage at Terrapin Crossroads, Phil turned Tiger over to guitarist Stu Allen, who played a soul-wrenching "Stella Blue."

"You know, the guitar was made to be played," Bobby told *Indianapolis Star* reporter David Lindquist. "Even if it someday ends up in a museum, I think half the time it should be trotted out and played, because that's what it was built to do. I know Jerry would feel that way."

Weir went on to tell Mr. Lindquist that "he'd be happy to hang out with Irsay."

Lindquist also reported, "Tiger has been displayed at the Indiana State Museum and the Eiteljorg Museum of American Indians and Western Art. Visitors to Irsay's office at Colts headquarters on 56th Street [in Indianapolis] can see Tiger displayed in a cabinet behind the owner's desk."

Mr. Irsay has been known to allow fans stopping by to play Tiger !

June 28, 2016

Who are Dead & Company and why do they keep following Donna Jean Godchaux ?

The only female member in the Grateful Dead's history has been greeted with humbling ovations during her guest appearances at several recent Dead & Co. shows, including both nights at CitiField this past weekend in Queens, NY, where Deadheads and concert-goers alike couldn't shower her with enough love.

It has always been my opinion that Donna — as well as Tom Constanten — should have been honored in Santa Clara and Chicago by being asked to sit in, even for a song or two, at the Dead's historic farewell concerts. It has been both remarkable, and no small joy, to see Ms. Godchaux onstage again alongside former-cohorts Weir, Kreutzmann and Hart, who made the magnanimous gesture of giving Donna the long-overdue props she deserves.

To Dead and Co.'s credit, and in an admirable display of generosity, the band first brought her out in front of 60,000 people at the Bonnaroo festival.

Welcome back to the big-time, Donna Jean !

Ms. Godchaux is one of eleven people, five of whom are deceased, who history will record as having been a performing member of the Grateful Dead. It's both exciting and a treat to see *any* four members of the Dead onstage together again, especially for Deadheads who never had the opportunity to see Donna with the band.

Like Bill Graham, Donna earned her own place in rock-n-roll history, separate from her achievements as a member of the Grateful Dead. She recalls the day she broke the news to Percy Sledge that "When a Man Loves a Woman" had hit the top of the charts: "Percy was in Helen Keller Hospital for treatment when Jeanie Greene and I took a copy of *Billboard* magazine into his room, and showed him that 'When a Man Loves a Woman' was No. 1 in the nation. What a memory that is. I will never forget it."

Donna's eight years in the Grateful Dead were marked by remarkable vocal work, both live and in the studio. Her vocals on Dead classics such as "Passenger" and "The Music Never Stopped" as well as her live work on songs such as "Playing in the Band" and "Cassidy" and, most notably, her psychedelic vocal scat during the segue from "Scarlet Begonias" to "Fire on the Mountain," are integral contributions to the Dead's studio and performing lore.

Most fans generally accept 1977 as the band's best live year and Donna was a key player on that team. She was also a member of the Jerry Garcia Band, and now she's getting her due with Dead & Co.

On Saturday, the CitiField crowd went ballistic when she was introduced before "Ramble on Rose." Donna was clearly moved. The next day, the band gave her a verse to sing during a ripping first-set "Going Down the Road Feeling Bad" — a great moment. I applaud Dead & Co. for welcoming Ms. Godchaux to their stage, for reuniting four members of the Grateful Dead in a live setting, and for giving numerous 'Heads both young and old the opportunity to hear Donna work her magic again.

August 16, 2016

Tom Constanten, who played on three Grateful Dead albums and was in the Dead for 14 months, fell on his way into the Post Office in his hometown near Charlotte, North Carolina and suffered a broken neck.

Mr. Constanten released the statement below.

Fell down and broke my neck last Wednesday.

Just like they warned me about as a kid.

I'd driven up to the Post Office at the top of the hill to mail off a bill, and, knowing there was heavy rain in the forecast, figured it would be better to mail it off inside. I parked the car, and on the way in a bit of uneven pavement tripped me up. I fell, face first, onto the concrete.

I am so very grateful for the woman who spotted me right away and called 911; for the ambulance crew, who got there so fast; for their professionalism and teamwork; for the uniformly excellent care at Novant Presbyterian Hospital; for the skill of Dr. Healy, the neurosurgeon who performed the procedure that pulled me out of the darkness and into the light, for Dr. Guignard, for the anesthesiologist, Dr. ... well, I'm spacing on his name, maybe because he did such a good job. For the surgeon who stitched up my forehead.

For the nurses, Beverly, Brooke, Brittany, Iseta, Julio, Cliff, Ali, Amelia.

I get back to the house, and the first thing I'm aware of is a forest of wonderful friends near and far showing such unbelievably warm support. I've experienced it before and, even though I have no idea what I might have done to deserve it, I felt the lift and reassurance.

The attitude of gratitude is in full bloom in this garden.

— Tom Constanten

August 18, 2016

Like John Mayer, former-major league baseball star and Cy Young Award winner Jake Peavy is new to being a Deadhead. "I think anyone who listens to music a lot gets exposed to the Grateful Dead at some point," he says.

This past May, when Jim Irsay lent Tiger to the Grateful Dead, Chris McKinney brought it first to Peavy (a close friend of Irsay's), who was key in convincing its owner to return Tiger to the wild.

Jake and a group of friends went to the first of the Dead's two Santa Clara shows in the summer of 2015. "Afterward, we were sitting around and saw online that Wolf and Tiger were going to be on display somewhere. And one of the guys said, 'Tiger is such an instrumental piece in the band's history and in Jerry's history. Wouldn't it be great to see it played onstage again ?'" Peavy told *Guitar Aficionado*, adding, "As Bobby said, 'It's what Jerry would have wanted.'"

Peavy, an Alabama native who won two World series titles before retiring in 2017, was traded to the San Francisco Giants in July, 2014. The trade became a life-altering event, as it wasn't long before the bus came by. Then-Giants third base coach Tim Flannery, an eleven-year big league vet and a bluegrass musician, introduced Jake to the Grateful Dead. "What really did it for me was going to Santa Clara," Peavy says. "That whole experience was unlike anything else. I was coming off a serious back injury, and the healing power of that music really saved me."

Although he wasn't planning to attend the second night, as the Giants had a flight that day to an away game, Jake, who wasn't scheduled to pitch for a few days, asked permission from Giants' manager Bruce Bochy, a "players' manager" who has led San Francisco to three World Series titles, to take a later flight so he could "join the party" on night two. Bochy had no problem with the request.

On the days Peavy pitched in 2016, he got to play deejay in the Giants' clubhouse. "Some of these younger guys don't quite know how to listen to it. I'm teaching them. We'll get there," he told SFGate.com.

Before a big game, it can be tight inside a locker room. "I'm trying to create the opposite of that vibe. I tell these guys, 'Let the Dead take you to a good place.'"

There were rumors that Mayer would play Tiger at the Dead & Co. show in Noblesville, Indiana but that didn't come to pass. "For a lot of reasons, [John] politely declined," Peavy explained to *Guitar Aficionado*. "Which I completely understand. He has some big shoes to fill, stepping into Jerry's role in that band. And he's not trying to be Jerry Garcia. He has his own sound."

When the Giants played at their home stadium, AT&T Park, in 2016, Peavy took the mound to "Truckin'." As he strode to the plate, the PA played "Shakedown Street."

Jake, who turns 36 in May, has won 152 games in his illustrious career and was on the inside track to the Hall of Fame before being derailed by injuries. His stellar run over, Peavy has already started down the road to a second career as a guitarist in the Outsiders, who shared a bill with Phil and Friends, the Trey Anastasio Band, and Jackie Greene at the Fillmore last August. "I made my major-league debut in front of 60,000 people and I've pitched in World Series games," he told the *Mercury News*, "but this is such a different energy, something I'd never experienced."

He picks at his guitar with the joy of a 12-year-old popping a baseball into a mitt. Looking up, he says, "The Dead, to me, is a way to be."

March 24, 2017

In a video of Bobby promoting his signature line of custom-built D'Angelico guitars, he discusses the time onstage he saw Jerry deeply in thought, playing a repetition of guitar "arpeggioed figures." When Bob walked over to Garcia, he claims Jerry was actually asleep onstage and playing in his sleep.

Now, that is what I call talent !

Bob, sharp in a grey suit, tears it up on his D'Angelico, performing solo versions of "Lay My Lily Down" and "Loose Lucy." He proclaims he "is just getting started," adding, "I put 30 years in with the Grateful Dead … [and] it all has to do with supporting the song."

With the camera focused closely on Weir's deep hazel eyes, he discusses mixing "Tennessee Jed" for *Europe '72* and how Phil described the sound of the D'Angelico guitar he played on the song as "a porcupine blowing kisses."

Bob says he took that as a compliment.

April 1, 2017

Jennifer Mydland is a budding singer/ songwriter whose on-stage debut took place this past Saturday night, April 1, at the Town Hall Theatre in Lafayette, CA, the hometown of her late dad — Brent.

In her brief four-song set, Ms. Mydland, 30, showed off her considerable vocal chops and blithe guitar stylings. Her voice is a compelling blend of a touch of Rickie Lee Jones, a dash of Janis and a whole lot of a young Shelby Lynne.

Jennifer kicked off with "I Don't Have You," following with a take on Amy Winehouse's "Valerie," which put her voice on full display as she pleaded: "Why don't you c'mon over and stop making a fool out of me."

Accompanied by electric guitarist Pat Nevins and keyboardist Scott Guberman, Ms. Mydland's playing moves with a touch of swing and is colored with beautiful rhythms and textures. Jennifer paid homage to the Grateful Dead with a cover of Kris Kristofferson's "Me and Bobby McGee," recorded by the Dead for their 1971 album, *Grateful Dead*.

At times nervous, Ms. Mydland did what Brent did best when he had those same pangs of uncertainty: confidently dive into the music. In a nearly-inaudible voice, she said, "Here we go !" before closing with a tribute to her father: an all-too-brief, but electrifying, take on "Dear Mr. Fantasy."

Proud older sister, Jessica, 33, looked on from the audience; it was Jessica whom Brent brought onstage to sit with him as he performed "I Will Take You Home" at Madison Square Garden in September, 1988.

I was truly impressed with Ms. Mydland's style and performing acumen and fell in love with her voice, finding myself wishing her set ran longer. I'd be really interested to hear her original material and see her play a longer show.

This young lady's star is going to zoom.

As with all things Grateful Dead, life continues to come full circle in the most profound, and moving, ways.

April 11, 2017

The Grateful Dead continue to be honored, and immortalized, in the strangest of places.

Major League Baseball stadiums, like movie theatres across America, have caught on to the fact that hosting a Grateful Dead tribute night at the ballpark will bring out Deadheads in droves.

More than a half-dozen major league teams, as well as a host of minor league teams, will hold Dead-themed nights during the upcoming 2017 season and some are offering ultra-cool, Dead-inspired perks and giveaways.

Among the teams honoring the Grateful Dead this spring and summer are the St. Louis Cardinals, Pittsburgh Pirates, Boston Red Sox, Philadelphia Phillies, Chicago White Sox (who brought out Tom Constanten last summer to throw out the traditional first pitch as part of their celebration), the Cincinnati Reds, who are giving away a Terrapin figurine, the Milwaukee Brewers, who are handing out an awesome Steal Your Face T-shirt, the hometown San Francisco Giants, and the Triple-A Richmond Flying Squirrels.

MLB teams are offering enticing incentives for Deadheads to attend. For starters, unlike most ballpark promotion nights, quality opponents are being scheduled. This summer, the Red Sox are hosting their division rival, the Baltimore Orioles, and the Pirates will tussle with the perennial NL power St. Louis Cardinals. Last summer, the White Sox played the New York Yankees and the Giants battled the New York Mets.

Both the Red Sox and Reds are handing out Dead-themed figurines. Some teams, such as the Red Sox, are making donations to the Rex Foundation while others, like the Brewers, have reached marketing agreements with the band's organization. The Brew Crew will be playing the Minnesota Twins on their Dead night — August 9, the 22nd anniversary of Jerry's passing. You may want to buy tickets now, as they are giving away an ultra-cool Steal Your Face T-shirt featuring an old-school Brewers logo in the "brain area."

So far, the most impressive Dead tribute night came on August 18, 2016 at the Giants' AT&T Park, where a very special guest was on hand: Tiger, who held a lengthy meet-and-greet with Deadheads and baseball fans alike.

Due to the overwhelming demand to meet Tiger, unfortunately, the ornate beauty was unable to sign autographs.

"The Giants are really married to the Grateful Dead family through things like [the tribute night], which [they] do at the ballpark," notes Jake Peavy.

Historic Fenway Park in Boston, the dwelling place for Red Sox Nation, will host their Grateful Dead night on April 11. The game versus the Orioles will feature a pre-game concert by Playing Dead, a Boston-based Dead cover band.

You never need an excuse to visit the shrine known as Fenway; on April 11, you'll have all the reason you need to venture to Boston. Buy a ducat to the game and you'll receive a limited edition Grateful Dead figurine — three dancing bears, one in a Sox uniform. As mentioned, the Red Sox will donate to the Dead's philanthropic wing, the Rex Foundation, named in honor of the late, and legendary, Grateful Dead stage technician and road manager, Donald "Rex" Jackson, who died in an automobile accident at age 31 in 1976.

(As of 2016. the Rex Foundation has awarded $8.2 million to more than 1,000 charities, causes and individuals since its 1983 inception.)

It's not just the Grateful Dead's music and ethos that continue to transform, shape and redefine American life and culture, it's the Deadhead fanbase as well.

As the movie theatres and ballparks are demonstrating, it's simple, and successful, socio-economics: Give Deadheads reason to gather, listen to Dead music, drink beer (even if it's expensive ballpark-priced suds), drop a few bucks, discreetly smoke up, and get sent home with a cool souvenir and we are down.

Soon enough, baseball will be changing the ageless lyrics of "Take Me Out to the Ballgame" to: "We'll root, root, root for the home team/ If they don't win, we'll smile, smile, smile" !

May 5, 2017

The Grateful Dead are now more commercially successful than at any point in their 30-year-history as a band, currently achieving unprecedented *Billboard* chart success.

May 1977: Get Shown The Light and *Cornell 5/8/77*, both released on May 5, simultaneously cracked *Billboard*'s Top 20 chart, only the Dead's fourth and fifth Top 20 albums ever, giving the group more Top 20 LPs in the past four years than during their entire 30-year reign !

In the post-Garcia era, the Grateful Dead are approaching Beatle-esque chart glory: This is the first time the Dead have had two albums in the Top 20 in the same week.

Cornell 5/8/77, an album of the Barton Hall concert, hit Number 10, just the second Grateful Dead album to reach the Top 10. *Blues for Allah*, which reached Number 12 in September, 1975, had been the band's second-highest charting album.

In September, 2013, *Sunshine Daydream*, a three-CD set of the Dead's show in Veneta on August 27, 1972, reached Number 19, giving the group their third Top 20 album and first since 1987, a span of 26 years.

In the Dark, released on July 6, 1987, is the Grateful Dead's best-selling and highest-charting album. On the strength of songs such as "Throwing Stones," "Tons of Steel" and the Dead's first and only Top 10 single — "A Touch of Grey" — the album peaked at Number 7 and the single at Number 9, leading one *Billboard* columnist to observe, "Good things come to those who wait."

"We [had] wondered if our true sound would ever be captured on record, whether the songs would ever be strong enough to pull through the studio torpor," said Weir after the success of *In the Dark*.

May 1977: Get Shown The Light, which features four complete Grateful Dead concerts from May of 1977 (New Haven on the 5th, the Boston Garden on the 7th, the Barton Hall show, and Buffalo on the 9th), peaked at Number 15 on the *Billboard* album chart.

Jerry would be equal parts proud, amused and horrified.

As he once famously said, "If you're able to enjoy something, to devote your life to it or a reasonable amount of time and energy, it will work out for you."

May 31, 2017

In 2002, Dan Pritzker purchased Garcia's beloved Wolf guitar during an auction in Manhattan.

Fifteen years later, Mr. Pritzker generously decided to auction Wolf, with the proceeds being awarded to the Southern Poverty Law Center in Montgomery, Alabama. The SPLC was founded in 1971 by Alabama businessman and lawyer Morris Dees, who specializes in civil rights law.

Pritzker, who has lent Wolf to, among others, Ryan Adams, Neal Casal and Warren Haynes to play, and the Rock and Roll Hall of Fame + Museum to exhibit, decided he wanted "Wolf to do some good."

At a Guernsey auction in Brooklyn on May 31, Wolf was sold for a lofty $1.9 million to Brian Halligan, a Deadhead, the co-founder and CEO of software company Hubspot, and a former venture capitalist.

Mr. Halligan's winning bid was $1.6 million (the auction house commission was $300,000), bringing the total to $1.9 million, which makes the Doug Irwin-crafted guitar one of the most-expensive rock-n-roll instruments ever purchased at auction.

"Two things I care deeply about: Jerry Garcia and social change," said Mr. Halligan afterward. "I am proud to support [the SPLC] with this donation."

Cooler yet: The $1.6 million bid was matched by another donor, bringing the total amount raised for the SPLC to an astonishing $3.2 million !

Well played, Brian !

The Wolf (along with the Travis Bean guitars) was one of Jerry's primary guitars onstage with the Grateful Dead from September, 1973 until July, 1979. In the summer of 1989, band technician Bob Bralove outfitted Wolf with MIDI capability and Garcia occasionally played the newly-updated guitar; beginning in September, 1989, he played Wolf more frequently until Rosebud was ready in 1990.

According to its webpage, the SPLC has "shut down some of the nation's most violent white supremacist groups ... dismantled vestiges of Jim Crow, reformed juvenile justice practices, shattered barriers to equality for women, children, the LGBT community and the disabled, and protected low-wage immigrant workers from exploitation."

Today, the SPLC provides a Teaching Tolerance program to "provide educators with free, anti-bias classroom resources such as classroom documentaries and lesson plans ... [and] reaches millions of schoolchildren with award-winning materials that teach them to respect others and help educators create inclusive, equitable school environments."

"If ever we needed the SPLC, we sure do need them now," said Mr. Pritzker.

June 4, 2017

Late in the second set of Dead & Company's stellar June 4 show at the Shoreline Amphitheatre, the band went on a run of "drums", "space", "The Other One", "A Hard Rain's a-Gonna Fall," the latter a Dylan song from *The Free Wheelin' Bob Dylan* (1963).

In these troubling times of turbulent politics, religious fanaticism and world-wide terrorism, Weir sang the tune with steely resolve. His voice captured the essence, and message, of the Dylan song and applied them to 2017: We are facing difficult days ahead that may result in catastrophic events.

Just a few nights earlier, on May 31, a bomb threat was called in during Dead and Co.'s show at the Hollywood Bowl in Los Angeles.

As the band was finishing "He's Gone" in the second set, the lights went dark and everyone was quickly escorted from the stage. The arena became eerily silent as a bomb-sniffing dog was brought out to patrol the stage area.

The show resumed several minutes later, with Bobby returning to the stage and commenting, "All clear ... kinda." The band then picked up with the "Like a steam locomotive ..." refrain from "He's Gone."

"A Hard Rain's a-Gonna Fall" was once described by a writer as "a complex and powerful song built upon the question-and-answer refrain pattern of the traditional [folk] ballad 'Lord Randall,'" which was published by Francis James Child in the late 19th century.

It's interesting to note that not only was Dylan influenced by Child, so was Robert Hunter. The Dead's wordsmith touched on the "grateful dead folk theme" — one of the oldest in religion, folklore, literature and music — in his lyrics, a theme that is featured throughout Child's five-volume collection, *The English and Scottish Popular Ballads* (1882-98).

Dylan and the Grateful Dead universe first crossed paths in 1961. Former-Merry Prankster Wavy Gravy was originally a comedian named Hugh Romney who managed the storied folk club the Gaslight Cafe in New York's Greenwich Village in 1961 and 1962. "I remember the night in 1961 when Dylan came in and asked me if he could go on and sing," recalls Wavy. "I said, 'What's your name, kid ?' He said, 'Bob Dylan.' And I grabbed the mic and said, 'Here he is folks, a legend in his own lifetime, Mr. Bob Dylan.'"

For a period, Dylan lived above the Gaslight with Wavy Gravy. "We shared a room for some time," reminisces Wavy. "He wrote 'A Hard Rain's a-Gonna Fall' on my typewriter."

Little did Dylan know that his song and its message of impending, and cathartic, change would be just as relevant almost 55 years after the night he wrote it above the Gaslight.

During their June 4 performance in an amphitheatre just a fog's roll from the Grateful Dead's hometown of San Francisco, Dead & Co. decided that "A Hard Rain's a-Gonna Fall" would be an appropriate song, and statement, to bring the evening, and another spectacular show, to a close.

June 11, 2017

In less than three short years, Dead & Company have clearly established themselves as the best Grateful Dead off-shoot band of the post-Garcia era, and by a wide margin. There is a level of musicianship, combined with a commitment to the music and culture, that is unsurpassed by every previous Grateful Dead incarnation dating to 1995.

Since Jerry passed away, we've seen talent-laden line-ups before — bands that have featured Trey Anastasio, Joe Russo, Jimmy Herring, Warren Haynes and Phil — but none have approached the level of commitment and passion that Dead & Co. bring to the stage each night. Like a basketball team that goes balls-to-the-wall for 48 minutes, Bobby and the gang let it all hang out at every show, leaving nothing on the court.

In the ever-evolving Grateful Dead hemisphere, this is, very likely, the last time we will see a Dead iteration grow and develop the way we have been blessed to watch Mayer & Co. mature. The past two summer tours have demonstrated how deep the band can take the music into the ether and entice the Mysterious Creature to become a nightly guest.

The experience is no different than watching Michael Jordan morph into an all-time great, one whose impact is so significant that, in your mind, there is no way anyone will ever come along and play in the same starry stratosphere.

And then LeBron James and Steph Curry come along.

The same thing holds true for the Grateful Dead and Dead & Co. After a lifetime of Jerry's wizardry, and the Dead's sorcery, it was unthinkable after Garcia died that any guitarist, or group, could come along and perform on that level again.

Or even close to it.

And then John Mayer and Dead & Co. come along.

The band brings the same ingredients to the table that the Grateful Dead brought to the table for 30 years: a good time in a healthy and diverse social and cultural environment with great music at the center of it all. When Dead & Co. are clicking on all cylinders, like the Dead, they serve as the 11th Gate, the golden pathway between Earth and heaven.

The difference between Dead & Co. and the other bands of the past 22 years is the wildly-gifted Mayer. The skinny kid from Connecticut, who Clapton rightfully labeled a "master," has proven Deadhead naysayers wrong while demonstrating he has the musical, emotional and intellectual gifts to next-level the Grateful Dead's music on a nightly basis.

In Mayer's voice, we hear the same cheer and optimism — along with traces of a familiar fragility — that emanated from Garcia's voice. In Mayer's guitar playing, there's a joy-infused energy similar to Jerry's playing, which Deadheads have been quick to feed off and react to in positive ways. "We live in a world where there's the comedy mask and the tragedy mask. It's either good or bad. You're either having a good day or a bad day," Mayer told *Rolling Stone* in 2017. "But then Grateful Dead music comes in, and it's this other mask. It's a third mask ... you [can] put on Grateful Dead music, which takes you to a completely different place. It inspires you, and it soothes you."

Dead & Co. mesh the way the Grateful Dead meshed. In doing so, they're able to abide by the edict Pigpen laid down as law: We play to serve the music and the fans, as the Dead did for thirty years.

Best, this summer Mickey and Billy and their four friends are providing Deadheads young and old with lifetime experiences. Is there anything more fun for us than to embark on a summer tour road trip to see a show or series of shows aware that the soft parade (and all its zaniness) known as Shakedown Street and two sets of great music await us at every gig ?

Not that I can think of.

Jerry summed up the on-the-road relationship between the Grateful Dead and Deadheads as only a person of his intelligence and wit could: "Essentially, the Grateful Dead audience is acting out their version of 'How much freedom is there left in America to go for a wild ride ?' It's hard to join the circus, and you can't hop the freights anymore, so you chase the Grateful Dead around. You can't be locked up for that yet.

"You have your adventures, when your car breaks down in Des Plaines and you need to hitchhike some place and a guy picks you up and he's a Deadhead. You can have your tires blown out in some weird town, and you get hell from strangers. These are your 'war stories.' You can have something that lasts through your life, the times you took chances.

"I think that's essential in anybody's life, and it's harder and harder to do in America. If we're providing some margin of that possibility [as well as] a safe context to be together with a lot of people who aren't afraid of each other, I guess we're important."

Garcia once used words to describe the Grateful Dead-Deadhead experience that can be applied to Dead & Company's state-side trek in the summer of '17: "[It's] one of the last adventures in America."

encores

June 21, 2017

By the 24th century, time will allow historians to look back at the Grateful Dead and use metaphysics to explain their success and popularity the way a mathematician uses numbers today to explain theorems. Until then, the Grateful Dead's legacy is that they, improbably, have a legacy at all.

They didn't sell a lot of records and garnered little radio airplay with, of course, the exception of the *In the Dark* period. To this day, the Dead remain the ultimate anomaly: disliked by legions but revered by legions more.

Two decades-plus after their disbandment, history's hand has judged Garcia and the Grateful Dead kindly.

And deservedly so.

Had Jerry lived, in my mind, an aged Garcia and Weir would have fronted the Grateful Dead, or a similar ensemble, into the 2010s and early 2020s, with the duo-led band having morphed into an acoustic configuration intentionally avoiding their own material in favor of bluesgrass, country and Dylan classics.

There is no doubt the Dead were defined by Jerry. You cannot have a larger-than-life figure in your rock-n-roll band, your business, or your family and not have that band, business or family defined by that person's considerable presence. This was, both blessedly and to his and the band's curse, the case with Garcia.

His success with the Grateful Dead was, in great part, attributable to the ability of Weir, Hart, Kreutzmann and Lesh — each masterful musicians in their own right — to stand alongside Jerry and play without ego. It's an easy concept to bandy about but, like most things in life, much more difficult to put into practice.

For one thing, it requires the ultimate sacrifice: putting aside your ego to not just serve the music but to back Garcia. That is what Phil, Bobby, Billy and Mickey, despite their individual musical gifts, did as well as any musician or group of musicians who have ever backed Jerry-level talent — from Coltrane and Paul Chambers standing behind Miles Davis to the E Street Band backing Bruce Springsteen.

Since Jerry "spun off the mortal coil," the remaining members of the Dead have done a truly remarkable job of keeping their band's music and culture alive. The ultimate testament to their perseverance is that their music, and its spirit, somewhat remarkably, and to their credit, has not just endured but flourished since 1995.

In addition to being a friend, bandmate and brother, the Dead recognized Garcia as a once-in-a-lifetime talent and personality, brilliant and gifted, music's Nikola Tesla, our Ben Franklin. And, in a very modest way, Jerry knew he was a rare bird. But intelligent people don't cry "look at me," they let their actions do their talking. There were few, if any, stage theatrics from Garcia when he played and, in the post-*Signpost to New Space* years, no major pronouncements in his interviews. His "big statements" were confined to, and hidden among, the notes he played and between the lines of the lyrics he sang.

Jerry was the physical manifestation of something greater than himself, greater than all of us, not only the jumper cables connecting the batteries of our world to the heavens but the spark plug as well.

He didn't just play the guitar and sing, he exuded beauty and emoted love. And, sometimes, the blues. That's why we loved him and why time continues to validate Garcia and the Grateful Dead. More than anything, Jerry was real, warts and all. He didn't hide who he was (nor should he have) and, had he tried, would have failed miserably. As sports writer Michael Bamberger once said of the golfer Arnold Palmer: "He never pretended to be something other than what he was."

In her eulogy at her father's wake, Annabelle Garcia lamented Jerry's parenting skills, which drew laughter from those who knew him well. She ended by adding, "He was a great guy."

August 25, 2017

On a brisk evening nestled among the Blue Ridge Mountains of Virginia, Bobby and Phil took the music of the Grateful Dead as far as it has ever been taken in the past 22 years by performing the entire "Terrapin Station Part 1" suite, replete with a "Jack O' Roses" ending, a monumental, and fitting, tribute to the poet Robert Hunter and a glorious moment in the history of the Grateful Dead and their music for Deadheads to cherish.

During the Phil Lesh and the Terrapin Family Band set at the Lockn' Festival in Arrington (pop. 703) on August 25, a soulful reading of "Stella Blue" by drummer Alex Kofford (beautifully complemented by the fiddle work of the austere Jason Crosby) was followed by Phil announcing, "Please welcome another dear friend."

Earlier in the set, Lesh had brought out his first guest (and dear friend) of the evening: Warren Haynes, who joined the Family Band for a romp through "St. Stephen" (that hinted at "Mountain Jam" during the song's bridge) and "Minglewood Blues."

The second "dear friend" turned out to be one of Phil's oldest: Bobby.

At that April, 1965 party in Palo Alto when Lesh and Weir met for the first time, the two stepped outside and smoked a "get-to-know-you" joint. Shortly thereafter, Phil was asked to join the Warlocks and, 52 years later, here they are at Lockn', still smoking.

Looking trim and fit in a black T-shirt and white pants, Weir led the band into the graceful opening of "Jack Straw;" the bridge jam was fueled by the fire of lead guitarist Ross James. An upbeat, and set-closing, "Uncle John's Band" followed that showed off Phil's cracker-jack crew. The anchor is drummer (and Lesh family cousin) Alex Kofford, who plays the fills and nuances of the Dead's music with subtlety and precision while also serving as an able vocalist.

At just past 11:30 p.m., the revolving stage turned clockwise to unveil Phil and Bobby (with vocalist Nicki Bluhm positioned between them); the duo led the Terrapin Family Band into "Estimated Prophet" and so began the band's much-awaited, and bally-hooed, performance of the *Terrapin Station* album, which was released 40 years ago this past July. Ross James shredded both the bridge solo and the exit jam.

"Dancing in the Streets" followed. Ms. Bluhm was truly stellar, as was Jason Crosby on keyboards. Bluhm then went shot for shot with Weir on the vocals during a smoking "Passenger" that featured sensational organ work from Crosby and a never-before-heard bridge sung by Weir and Bluhm featuring the lyrics "pour me one more whiskey."

Bluhm's outstanding work, especially on the "Samson and Delilah" that came next, demonstrated the importance of Donna Jean Godchaux to both the *Terrapin Station* album and the Grateful Dead. Needless to say, Nicki was equal to the daunting task when it came time to sing Donna's "Sunrise." She showed great range and vocal depth and the Godchaux number became another of the evening's outstanding moments, with Phil appearing ecstatic at how well the song came off.

"Terrapin Station Part 1," which is how the song is titled on the album, was sung by Bob. The oeuvre is a seven-piece movement on the LP and was never performed in its entirety by the Grateful Dead.

Would Phil, Bobby, Nicki and the Terrapin Family Band change that on this cool mountain evening ?

Phil could hardly contain his excitement as he sang the post-"Inspiration" lyrics in unison with Bob, Ms. Bluhm and the TFB vocalists.

I was shocked when Weir and Ross James led the band into "Terrapin Transit" and delirious as Bobby sang "At a Siding":

"The compass always points to Terrapin."

Alex Kofford steered the ensemble through "Terrapin Flyer" as James riffed on the guitar; the music, and this moment, were both timeless and overbubbling with excitement. Crosby contributed a number of Chick Corea-like runs on the keyboards.

One of the most surprising, and thrilling, moments in Grateful Dead lore followed: a compelling performance of Robert Hunter's "Jack O' Roses," sung with great conviction by Grahame Lesh.

In Hunter's annotated lyric collection, *A Box of Rain*, he writes: "'Jack O' Roses' [is an example] of subsequent attempts to complete the ['Terrapin' lyric] cycle. [The 'Jack O' Roses' lyrics] are included [in *A Box of Rain*] as part of the ['Terrapin'] suite since they do have pieces of the resolution within them."

As Grahame sang Hunter's tale, it felt as if a chapter was being closed in the grand story of the Grateful Dead, with no new one to move on to.

Close to 12:30 a.m., the song was both sad and beautiful:

Terrapin
if anyone should ask of you who made this
    song
say the Jack O' Roses and all who played
    along
who rise, climb, fall to win
Terrapin

July 7, 2089

Inevitably, one day a nondescript headline will run atop the back page of one of the world's last-surviving print newspapers: "Last living Deadhead to see Grateful Dead with Garcia dies."

Beneath it, an obituary will read:

Estelle Katherine Joseph, 94, known as "Katie Mae" to her friends in the Bend, Oregon community where she spent her entire life, passed away on July 7, 2089 of natural causes. She was ten months old when her parents took her to see the Grateful Dead on May 29, 1995 at the Portland Meadows.

Born August 1, 1994, Ms. Joseph was 18 and a recent Bend High School graduate when she accepted a summer internship at Algae Systems, LLC, a Nevada energy and utility company specializing in cost-effective non-fossil fuels. Co-founded in 2011 by her boss, civil libertarian John Barlow, it was only after calling home to tell her parents about her first day at work that she learned her boss had had a previous career as a lyricist for the Grateful Dead.

Joseph and Barlow spent the next decade turning Algae Systems into an international non-fossil fuel corporate giant, effectively putting an end to the fossil fuel industry. *The New York Times* noted: "By 2025, Ms. Joseph and Mr. Barlow had tossed the last shovelful of dirt on the industry and once thought to be invincible mega-conglomerates Exxon, Mobil and British Petroleum."

In 2031, Joseph left Algae to found Birdsong Energy, which earned world-wide repute for using carbon-capture technology to remove carbon from the air in low-income housing, inner-city schools, and urban activity centers, hiring local residents to assist with the work. Birdsong would then convert the extracted carbon into eco-friendly, non-fossil fuel and donate it back to the same neighborhoods for use in schools and small businesses. "The wheel is turning and it can't slow down," Ms. Joseph proudly said of her business model.

Katie Mae, as she preferred to be called, served as founder, president and CEO of Birdsong for 52 years. Its headquarters, situated in Bend, employs as many as 85% of the town's citizens. In 2039, Katie came up with the visionary concept of the work-place Marijuana Break, a half-hour respite that allows employees, who are later bussed home, to smoke marijuana in an outdoor company park. The Marijuana Break pushed Birdsong's production through the roof and it wasn't long before the work-day timeout become an integral part of the American workplace and landscape. "A happy worker is a more productive, imaginative, and focused worker," she boasted.

A University of Oregon graduate among the first awarded a Ph. D. in metaphysics, Ms. Joseph is also a multiple Nobel recipient and a Pulitzer winner. Her parents arrived early at the meadows to see the opening act, another guitar legend: Chuck Berry. Katie had no conscious recollection of her first and only Grateful Dead concert but was quoted as saying, "Something magical happened that night in that meadow in Portland that I cannot put into words. My parents told me I had been asleep for most of the evening but opened my eyes and smiled at them during 'Terrapin Station.'"

Of the Grateful Dead, Katie Mae once observed, "On its highest levels, my relationship with the Grateful Dead has helped to shape my God concept and developed, and mediated, my relationship with God. It made me believe in the stuff of a utopian world: love, kindness, mercy, empathy, sympathy, joy, ecstasy, forgivingness, understanding."

Ms. Joseph narrowly edged writer Scott W. Allen (who had passed away only days earlier) for the distinction of being the last living Deadhead to have seen the Grateful Dead with guitarist Jerry Garcia.

Appendix

Resources

Articles — online and print

"8 Disturbing Facts About Tupac Shakur"
by Josh Rindskopf
CheatSheet.com
June 19, 2017

"A Heavenly Goodbye to a Hells Angels in 1960s San Francisco"
by Bill Van Niekerken
SFChronicle.com
June 6, 2016

"Branford Marsalis on His Unlikely Collaboration with the Grateful Dead"
by David Fricke
RollingStone.com
July 10, 2014

"Chronicles of the Dead"
by Rock Scully and David Dalton
Playboy
December 1995

"*Don't Let Go*, by Jerry Garcia"
by Stephen Rose
TheListeningPost.TotallyGuitars.com
February 19, 2014

"From Eternity to Here"
by Charles Perry
Rolling Stone
February 26, 1976

"Garcia and Let It Be Telecaster"
by Andy Babiuk
CheapStrat.com
January 25, 2015

"George Harrison's Fender Rosewood Telecaster
'Rooftop Concert' Guitar Was Bought By Ed Begley Jr."
by Raul
FeelNumb.com
December 10, 2010

"Giants' Jake Peavy mellows out to Grateful Dead"
by John Shea
SFGate.com
August 9, 2015

"GRATEFUL DEAD CONCERT IS FREE AND OPEN-AIR"
Wesleyan Argus
May 1, 1970
(reprinted from DeadEssays.BlogSpot.com)

"Grateful Dead live on in alumni memories of Barton Hall '77"
by Daniel Aloi
www.news.cornell.edu/stories
February 9, 2010

"How Jerry Garcia Revolutionized the Custom Guitar Industry
in His Pursuit of Excellence"
by Chris Gill
GuitarAficionado.com
April 22, 2014

"Jake Peavy, SF Giants pitcher and Deadhead: 'Too grateful to be hateful'"
by *Marin Independent Journal* and Paul Libertore
MercuryNews.com
August 5, 2016

"Jerry Garcia and the Pedal Steel Guitar"
by Crusader Cob
No Depression — The Journal of Roots Music
NoDepression.com
August 20, 2012

"Jerry's Secrets"
by Robert Greenfield
Jerry Garcia: The Ultimate Guide to His Music & Legend
Rolling Stone Special Collector's Edition
2014

"Jim Irsay sends Garcia's guitar to visit Dead & Company"
by David Lindquist
IndyStar.com
May 23, 2016

"John Mayer, Dead & Co. take weed tour while touring Colorado"
TheCannibist.com
November 23, 2015

"John Mayer Talks Grateful Dead Legacy, Fare Thee Well and Learning to Play 'A Universe of Great Songs'"
by Shirley Halperin
Billboard
August 5, 2015

"Leilani Münter — Environmentalist-Vegetarian Race Car Driver"
Midweek.com
by Chad Pata
December 5, 2008

"Love Is Just a Song We Sing but a Contract Is Something Else"
by Ben Fong-Torres
Rolling Stone
February 26, 1976

"On a Roll"
by Fred Goodman
Jerry Garcia: The Ultimate Guide to His Music & Legend
Rolling Stone Special Collector's Edition
2014

"Paul McCartney, Beatle and Deadhead Director"
by Neil Strauss
NYTimes.com
September 26, 1996

"Phil Lesh 'Not Completely There Yet' Processing Jerry Garcia's Death"
by David Fricke
Rolling Stone
April 21, 2014

"Supporter to auction legendary Grateful Dead guitar to benefit SPLC"
SPLCCenter.org
March 31, 2017

"The Dead experience: Band connections abound in Northeastern Pennsylvania"
by Matt Mattei
The Times Leader (PA)
December 18, 2016

"The Last Word: Bob Weir on Grateful Dead's Legacy, Adele, Fame's Downside"
by David Browne
Rolling Stone
October 25, 2016

"The Last Word: Phil Lesh on Favorite Jerry Garcia Memory, Love for Sci-Fi
by David Fricke
Rolling Stone
August 17, 2016

"The Music Never Stops"
by Anthony DeCurtis
Jerry Garcia: The Ultimate Guide to His Music & Legend
Rolling Stone Special Collector's Edition
2014

"Racing on Sunshine with Leilani Münter"
PVSolarReport.com
September 16, 2014

"Storytime: 'The Mime Speaks'"
by David Wexler
JanglingSouls.com
April 11, 2015

APPENDIX

"Surprise announcement recalls the year Grateful Dead played West High auditorium"
by Chris Bieri
Alaska Dispatch News
ADN.com
March 16, 2017

"Video: Grateful Dead on 'Saturday Night Live' — 1980"
by Scott Bernstein
GlideMagazine.com
January 31, 2013

"Warren Haynes Gives Jerry Garcia's Tiger Guitar an Encore Turn"
by Richard Bienstock
GuitarAficionado.com
October 5, 2016

"Watch: Warren Haynes Details 'Spots of Time' Written with Phil Lesh"
by Rob Slater
Relix.com
June 1, 2015

"When the Grateful Dead came to town: A quick history of the band's Minnesota trips"
by Jesse Jarnow
CityPages.com
May 5, 2017

"Weir finds his birth father and adopts a vintage guitar"
by Joel Selvin
SFGate.com
March, 2004

Articles — online (with links)

"[An] Interview with Doug Irwin —
The man who crafted Jerry's guitars"
by SQ
Dozin.com
2009

http://dozin.com/dougirwin/interview.html

"Charles George 'Chocolate George' Hendricks"
by C & N Rasmussen
FindAGrave.com
April 10, 2011

https://www.findagrave.com/cgi-bin/fg.cgi?page=gr&GRid=68144964

"Donna Jean Godchaux on Meeting and Recording with Elvis Presley"
Rock and Roll Hall of Fame + Museum
July 20, 2012

https://www.youtube.com/watch?v=Kl8WddfHcR0

"Garcia's Cripes | Lightning Bolt"
Cripe Guitars Tribute
CripeGuitars.com

http://www.cripeguitars.com/bolt.html

"Grateful Dead Guide — An ongoing series of articles on
songs & performances of the early Grateful Dead"
by Light Into Ashes
DeadEssays.BlogSpot.com
2013

http://deadessays.blogspot.com/2013/02/may-3-1970-wesleyan-university.html

APPENDIX

"'Haul' of Fame Interview with 'Fluff' Cowan"
Caddy Bytes — An "inside the ropes" look at tournament golf
CaddyBytes.com
2003

http://www.caddybytes.com/fluff_cowan!.htm

"How 'long and quiet' nights on the ranch inspired Bob Weir's new album"
"CBS This Morning: Saturday"
© 2016 CBS Interactive Inc.
All rights reserved.

Interview conducted by Anthony Mason.

http://www.cbsnews.com/news/bob-weir-grateful-dead-founding-member-new-album-blue-mountain-inspiration/

"Jerry Garcia guitar history"
Dozin.com

http://dozin.com/jers/guitar/history.htm

"Chapter Two: Recall the Days That Still Are to Come"
by Blair Jackson
BlairJackson.com

http://www.blairjackson.com/chapter_two_additions.htm

"Stephen Ray Cripe 1954 — 1996"
Dozin.com

http://www.dozin.com/jers/guitar/bolt.html

"Super kind Jerry Garcia throws Lesh down stairs"
YouTube.com
posted by Tito Garcia
September 15, 2010

https://www.youtube.com/watch?v=jxKdYS90qIA

"The San Francisco Diggers"
The Digger Archives
Diggers.org

http://www.diggers.org/ringolevio/ring444.html

"Top Women Race Car Drivers"
SI.com/Racing
March 21, 2007

http://www.si.com/racing/photos/2007/03/21-0top-women-race-car-drivers

Books

A Box of Rain — Collected Lyrics of Robert Hunter
by Robert Hunter
Viking Penguin
New York, NY (1990)

Aces Back to Back: The History of the Grateful Dead (1965 — 2015)
by Scott W. Allen
Outskirts Press
Parker, CO (2013)

Conversations with the Dead — The Grateful Dead Interview Book
by David Gans
Citadel Press
New York, NY (1991)

DeadBase, Jr.: The Portable Guide to Grateful Dead Song Lists
by John W Scott, Mike Dolgushkin and Stu Nixon
DeadBase
Hanover, New Hampshire (1995)

Deal: My Three Decades of Drumming, Dreams,
and Drugs with the Grateful Dead
by Bill Kreutzmann with Benjy Eisen
St. Martin's Press
New York, NY (2015)

Garcia: An American Life
by Blair Jackson
Penguin Books
London, UK (1999)

Richard Condon
by David Willis McCullough
Mysterious Press
New York, NY (1988)

Searching for the Sound: My Life with the Grateful Dead
by Phil Lesh
Little, Brown and Company
New York, NY (2005)

Film

Citizen Kane
directed by Orson Welles
RKO Radio Pictures
1941

Festival Express
directed by Bob Smeaton
THINKFilm
2003

Long Strange Trip
directed by Amir Bar-Lev
Amazon Video
January 23, 2017

The Manchurian Candidate
directed by John Frankenheimer
United Artists
October 24, 1962

The Saragossa Manuscript
directed by Wojciech Has
Film Polski
February 9,1965

The Other One: The Long, Strange Trip of Bob Weir
directed by Mike Fleiss
Next Entertainment
2014

Magazine compendiums

Jerry Garcia: The Ultimate Guide to His Music & Legend
Rolling Stone Special Collector's Edition
© Wenner Media Specials
2014

"What a Long Strange Trip It's Been —
San Francisco Ten Years On"
Issue No. 207
Rolling Stone
February 26, 1976

Podcasts

"Weir Here"
#13
directed by Justin Kreutzmann
March 13, 2013
© TRI Studios

https://www.youtube.com/watch?v=jfPGwJZ9-1g

Television

"The Movie That Changed My Life"
© AMC
1995

https://www.youtube.com/watch?v=qeW-kdQ46ys&list=PL929111454AAC0664

Websites

Archive.org
BlairJackson.com
CripeGuitars.com
DeadEssays.BlogSpot.com
Dead.net
Dictionary.com
Dozin.com
GuitarAficionado.com
Jambase.com
JerryGarcia.com
Phish.net
PVSolarReport.com
RollingStone.com
SFChronicle.com
TheGuardian.com
Thesaurus.com
Wikipedia.com
YouTube.com

Unsourced materials

"1966 Interview with the Grateful Dead"
AngelFire.com

http://www.angelfire.com/fl/goodbear/interview66.html

Wikipedia

Source material for the essay "May 1, 1941" was found on Wikipedia.com at:

https://en.wikipedia.org/wiki/Citizen_Kane

Source material for the essay "1972" was found on Wikipedia.com at:

https://en.wikipedia.org/wiki/The_Manchurian_Candidate

Source material for the essay "Fall, 1990" was found on Wikipedia.com at:

https://en.wikipedia.org/wiki/Tupac_Shakur

Source material for the essay "2008" was found on Wikipedia.com at:

https://en.wikipedia.org/wiki/Leilani_Munter

Source material for the essay "June 4, 2017" was found on Wikipedia.com at:

https://en.wikipedia.org/wiki/A_Hard_Rain%27s_a-Gonna_Fall

Songs to Fill the Air:
Tales of the Grateful Dead

Cover illustration

Steve Johannsen
JohannsenStudio@gmail.com
Steves-Art.com

Editor

Erik Anderson
swollenfamous@gmail.com

Interior Illustrations

Hannah Hopkins
GiveAPaintBrush@gmail.com
RockMySoulArt@gmail.com

<u>**Graphic Design and Manuscript Formatting**</u>

Outskirts Press

Brie Curtis
Author Representative

Heidi Jones
Revision Specialist

Lisa Jones
Author Representative

Tina Ruvalcaba
Publishing Consultant

This book was written using pencil, pen and paper, a typewriter, MicroSoft Word, and Adobe InDesign CS6.

Copyrights and Permissions

Songs to Fill the Air: *Tales of the Grateful Dead*
© 2017
Scott W. Allen

All rights reserved. No part of this publication may be reproduced or transmitted in any form or by any means (electronic or otherwise), in part or in whole, including serializations, without the prior expressed written permission of the publisher and the author.

Cover Illustration
© 2017
Steve Johannsen

All rights reserved. Reprinted by permission. No part of the cover illustration may be reproduced or transmitted in any form or by any means (electronic or otherwise), in part or in whole, without the prior expressed written permission of both the artist and the publisher. The cover image is owned by and copyrighted by Steve Johannsen.

Inquiries welcome:

JohannsenStudio@gmail.com

Interior Illustrations
© 2017
Hannah Hopkins

All rights reserved. Reprinted by permission. No part of the ten (10) interior illustrations on pages 7, 18, 34, 38, 88, 106, 117, 121, 138 and 169 may be reproduced or transmitted in any form or by any means (electronic or otherwise), in part or in whole, without the prior expressed written permission of both the artist and publisher. The ten (10) interior illustrations, as listed above, are owned by and copyrighted by Hannah Hopkins.

Inquiries welcome:

GiveAPaintBrush@gmail.com
RockMySoulArt@gmail.com

"I can envisage a new world in which society has a way for there to be music, whose function is to get you high. That's the sort of thing we're hammering at."

— Jerry

Dedicated with thanks to my brother, Chris, my concert partner-in-crime and best friend.

Special thanks and love

Marilyn and Anthony D'Aria, Cindy and Derek, Chris and Anthony
Hannah Hopkins, Andrea Robbins, Steve Johannsen and Erik Anderson
Paul, Lynda, Debbi and Adriana and families
the good folks at Outskirts Press
Rhonda Turso
Stephen Bykowsky
Glen Troiano and Scott D. Rhodes
the Grateful Dead and Deadhead community
Christopher Bandini, Frank Pietrzak, Robert Pistella
Anthony Renna, Garth Flanders, Tim Parker
Lennon Blachly, Robin Russell, Billy Birke, Scott Rudicel
Matthew Furzland, Bob Hoeler, Peter David, Marc H. Arbeeny
Dan Meszler, Catherine McNaughton, Jim Halvorson, John LeClair
Rock Stamberg, Moss Willow, Bill Stiner, Thomas L. Qualley, Keith Welch
Jim Klumper, Mark B. Levy, Mark Murgittroyd, Chris Enstad, Mike Hollander
Joseph G. Lewis, Bruce Johnson, Brendan Sheehan, Jeff Trudeau, David Holmes
the Jaspen family
Justin Vail, Ross Patane
John and Susan Caldwell
Steve Goldston and family
Paula Hamilton and the girls
John Zubler and Jason Zubler
Matt, Bridger and Norah Boucher
Nicholas Szumylo and Keitha Mahon
Brent, Lisa, Sierra and Sage Holverson ~NFA~
Shelly Stevens, Patrick Murphy, William Kirkwood
Bette Tropek-Miller, Eric Coughlin, Jenni Bryant, Tim Dwyer
Gregory Andersen, Brian Corwin, Roger Bodian, Michael Chasse
Norman Jaffe, Thomas Ganley, John Jamieson, Stephen Gilmour
Erik Sowa, Andrew Grubbs, Chris Dupuis, Sean Callahan, Tim Dwyer
Casey Pond, Dan and Shannon Zehr, John Marshall, Peter Ferioli, Kristina Isaacs
Daniel Jones, Linda Forisso-Corbly, Jessica Curtis, Moreyn Kamenir, Jason Gould
William P. Provost, Larry Ward, Rob Perrin, Dennis Koessel, Ana Ceberg Fleming, Marty Katz
Marci Strouch, Kevin Magee, Jay Wolk, Scott Allen, Brian Michaelson, Chris Elliott, Trace DeHaven
Sean Goldfarb, Ryan "Steal Your Face" Miraglia, Jon Moulesong, Jim Cockerham, Douglas Emerson
John Abate, Kareem, Tommy A., Bones, Leony, Gus, Mike Kennedy, Mike G., Chris Bell, Mike Dowd
Bronx, Julius, Joe P., Danny, Mike Despo, John Despo, Enzo, Steve Becker, Ian Wilson, Butch

Hannah Hopkins would like to thank

My wonderful mother, Andrea Robbins
Thomas Laurance Photography
Matty Barca
Erin Lippert & Bill Batson of FOJC
Donald Darwin, Bruce Grossman